Entenmann's

BIG BOOK OF BAKING

Entenmann's®

BIG BOOK OF BAKING

First published in 2011

ISBN: 978-1-4454-4530-4

Parragon
Queen Street House
4 Queen Street
Bath
BA1 1HE, UK

Printed in China

The times given are approximate guide only. Cooking times may
vary depending on the type of oven used. All spoon measurements
are level. Unless otherwise stated milk is assumed to be whole and
eggs are large. Some recipes specify self rising flour. If you do not
have self rising flour all-purpose flour can be used. For each cup
of all-purpose flour, add 1½ teaspoons of baking powder and
½ teaspoon of salt. People with nut allergies should be aware that
some of the prepared ingredients used in the recipes in this book
may contain nuts. Always check the packaging before use.

Contents

Almost Homemade   8

Donuts, Danish & Puffs   90

Crumb Cakes   112

Muffins   124

Loaf Cakes   150

Brownies & Bars   184

Cookies   218

Pies   240

Indulgent Cakes & Desserts   270

Party Cakes   300

Index   318

Introduction

For the past 23 years, I have worked at Entenmann's Bakery, where I've had the pleasure of helping to research and develop scores of delectable Entenmann's baked goods. After majoring in Food Science in College and working for years as a hands-on baker, today I am a "Master Baker", whose enviable job is to innovate, develop, and refine baked goods for the Entenmann's brand.

As you might imagine, this job involves lots of testing for quality control and lots of tasting! So I'm very excited to bring that expertise to the recipes in this book, assuring that each of the recipes included here works perfectly for every home baker and tastes absolutely delicious.

Entenmann's history goes back over 110 years to 1898 when William Entenmann opened his first bakery in Brooklyn, New York. By the 1960s, the company was selling throughout the New York Metropolitan area, and by the 1970s, it began selling nationwide. Today, Entenmann's markets over 100 different baked goods across the United States. These include such Entenmann's classics as Rich Frosted Donuts, Chocolate Chip Cookies, a variety of coffee and crumb cakes such as Raspberry Danish Twist, and, of course, Entenmann's All Butter Loaf Cake, which has been part of the bakery's repertoire since its inception in 1898, and has sold over 700 million cakes to date.

At Entenmann's, we often describe our baked goods as "indulgent", which to us means not only luxurious and perhaps a bit sinful—but rich, sweet and of course, delicious! In addition to the emphasis on decadent flavors, we also pay attention to portion control and convenience. Toward that end, we've created a line of Little Bites and Mini-Cakes, which are small, individually wrapped portions of our most popular baked goods that are perfect to enjoy on the go. No matter what the size, all Entenmann's products are baked with real ingredients – real apples and raspberries, and real grade A butter for example, to deliver the highest level of quality and flavor in every bite.

With The Entenmann's Big Book of Baking, anybody who loves to bake—old or young, experienced baker or busy amateur—can now make Entenmann's inspired baked goods at home. It features over 140 mouth-watering recipes, including many that will remind you of Entenmann's classics, such as Chocolate Chip Cookies and some interesting new ideas, such as a Blackberry & Apple Loaf Cake recipe. There are recipes for every occasion, from a leisurely Sunday morning breakfast treat to a child's special birthday cake, or the ultimate crowd-pleasing Double Chocolate Brownies.

Also included are creative recipe suggestions for using a few simple ingredients with your favorite Entenmann's product to create home-style desserts in a fraction of the time. For example, try pouring warm chocolate sauce over Entenmann's Little Bite Fudge Brownies or serving a sweet syrup or fresh fruit with slices of toasted Entenmann's All-Butter Loaf for a delicious snack or dessert.

Well-tested, great tasting, and crowd-pleasing—The Entenmann's Big Book of Baking will inspire the baker in you! Rich, sweet, and delicious! Enjoy!

Kathleen Robbins

Master Baker
Entenmann's Bakery

Almost Homemade

Almond Slices

Makes 8 slices

1 Entenmann's All Butter Loaf Cake

2 tablespoons maple syrup

1 tablespoon brandy

1 cup sugar

1 cup sliced almonds

1 teaspoon salt

6 tablespoons butter, softened

2 eggs

Confectioners' sugar for dusting

Directions

- Preheat the oven to 350°F.

- Line a baking sheet with parchment paper.

- Slice the Entenmann's All Butter Loaf Cake into 8 slices and lay on the baking sheet.

- In a small bowl mix together the maple syrup and the brandy. Brush generously onto the 8 slices of cake.

- Combine the sugar, ⅔ cup of sliced almonds, and salt in the bowl of a food processor.

- Process until finely ground, then add the butter and process for a further 10 seconds. Slowly add in the eggs and process until the mixture is creamy.

- Spoon 3 tablespoons of the almond filling across each of the slices. Sprinkle with the remaining almonds.

- Bake for 15-20 minutes, until the almond cream is firm and the sliced almonds are golden.

- Serve for breakfast or dessert, dusted with confectioners' sugar.

You can use the Entenmann's Loaf Cake suggested or any of our classic selections or seasonal Loaf Cake favorites to make this recipe: All Butter, Marble, Chocolate Chip, Raisin, Sour Cream, Lemon, Cranberry Orange or Banana.

Yummy Rummy Fruit Parfait

Serves 4

1 Entenmann's All Butter Loaf Cake

2 cups frozen whipped topping, thawed

3 cups assorted fresh berries such as
blueberries, strawberries or raspberries

1 cup canned or fresh pineapple chunks
(optional)

4 tablespoons rum (optional) or

2 tablespoons chocolate fudge sauce

Fresh mint for garnish

Directions

• Cut the Entenmann's All Butter Loaf Cake, into 1-inch cubes and sprinkle lightly with the rum or chocolate fudge sauce.

• Puree one cup of the berries in a food processor or blender.

• In an individual glass alternate the cake chunks with the processed berries, whipped topping and fresh fruit.

• Top with the whipped topping.

• Decorate with a mint leaves and serve immediately.

You can use the Entenmann's Loaf Cake suggested or any of our classic selections or seasonal Loaf Cake favorites to make this recipe: All Butter, Marble, Chocolate Chip, Raisin, Sour Cream, Lemon, Cranberry Orange or Banana.

Coffee Toffee Ice Cream Pie

Serves 8-10

One package Entenmann's Chocolate Chip
cookies of any variety

6 tablespoons butter, melted

1 pint coffee ice cream

¼ cup broken toffee pieces or toffee
chips

Directions

• Preheat the oven to 350°F. Grease a 9-inch pie pan.

• In a food processor, process the cookies until they
are crumbs.

• Pour the crumbs into a large bowl and mix with the
melted butter. Press the mixture firmly into the
bottom of the pan.

• Bake for 20 minutes, until the edges are brown and
the crust is golden.

• Remove from the oven and use a spatula or back
of a spoon to press down, deflating the crust.
Cool completely.

• Sprinkle 2 tablespoons of the broken toffee pieces
on top of the crust.

• Allow the ice cream to soften for 10 minutes before
spreading evenly into the crust using a spatula
dipped in warm water to make a smooth surface.

• Sprinkle the remaining toffee bits across the top.

• Wrap tightly with plastic wrap and put in the
freezer for at least 2 hours.

• Decorate with broken cookie pieces or broken
toffee pieces.

Fruit Cobbler

Serves 6-8

1 Entenmann's Ultimate Crumb Cake

4 cups frozen or canned peach slices

1½ cups frozen blueberries

2 tablespoons sugar

Juice from 1 lemon

Directions

- Preheat the oven to 350°F.

- Grease a 9x9-inch square baking dish.

- Toss together the fruit, sugar, and lemon juice and leave to soak for 10 minutes.

- Bake for 25 minutes, until the fruit has released most of its juice.

- Slice the Entenmann's Ultimate Crumb Cake into squares and spread evenly across the top of the fruit base.

- Return to the oven and bake for 15-20 minutes, until the tops of the crumb cake are golden, and the fruit has lost its shape.

- Allow to rest for 15-20 minutes before serving warm, with ice cream.

*You can use the Entenmann's Crumb Cake suggested or any of our classic selections or seasonal favorites to make this recipe: Classic, Ultimate, Butter French or New York Style Crumb Cake.

Little Bites Brownie Surprise

Serves 4-6

1 package Entenmann's Little Bites
Brownies

1 tub of frozen whipped topping, thawed

1 pack (6 cups) prepared chocolate pudding

2 chocolate coated toffee candy bars

½ cup toffee chips

Directions

• Break up the Entenmann's Little Bites Brownies into small 1-inch pieces and cover the bottom of a large glass bowl.

• Add a layer of prepared chocolate mousse and cover with a layer of whipped topping.

• Top the whipped topping with broken up pieces of a candy bar.

• Add another layer of brownies, chocolate mousse and whipped topping.

• Refrigerate for a minimum of 2 hours.

• Top with a sprinkling of broken up candy pieces and toffee chips just before serving.

S'more Party Cups

Serves 4

12 Entenmann's Little Bites Brownies, crumbled

½ cup milk chocolate, broken into pieces

8 chocolate coated graham crackers broken into pieces

¾ cup marshmallow crème

Directions

- Melt the chocolate pieces in a glass dish placed over a pan of simmering water.

- Spoon the melted chocolate into four foil cupcake liners spreading the chocolate on bottom and up the sides with a pastry brush or back of a small spoon.

- Place in a refrigerator to chill. When the chocolate has set, carefully peel away and discard the foil liners.

- To assemble, spread a teaspoon of marshmallow crème into the bottom of each chocolate cup.

- Divide the crumbled Entenmann's Little Bites Brownies among the cups and top with the remaining marshmallow crème.

- Finally crush the chocolate coated graham crackers and sprinkle on the top of each cup.

- Serve immediately or store in the refrigerator.

Almond Chocolate Biscotti

Serves 12-14 pieces

1 Entenmann's All Butter Loaf Cake

¼ cup milk chocolate chips, melted

¼ cup white chocolate chips, melted

2 tablespoons sliced almonds

Directions

- Preheat oven to 350°F. Lightly grease a baking sheet.

- Slice one Entenmann's All Butter Loaf Cake in half lengthwise. Then slice each half into 1 inch thick slices. creating 14 slices.

- Carefully place the slices on the baking sheet. Bake in the oven for 10 minutes. Turn the oven off, and let the biscotti remain in the oven for an additional 15-18 minutes until they are crisp and golden brown.

- Remove from oven and allow to cool.

- Melt the milk chocolate chips in a glass bowl placed over a saucepan of simmering water or in short bursts in a microwave.

- Drizzle some of the melted milk chocolate over the biscotti with a fork. Repeat with the melted white chocolate.

- Sprinkle almond slivers over melted chocolate. Drizzle more of both chocolates over the almonds and allow to set.

- Serve immediately or store in an airtight container. The dry biscotti will keep for several weeks.

*You can use the Entenmann's Loaf Cake suggested or any of our classic selections or seasonal Loaf Cake favorites to make this recipe: All Butter, Marble, Chocolate Chip, Raisin, Sour Cream, Lemon, Cranberry Orange or Banana.

Cookie Sour Cream Coffee Cake

Serves 8-10

Batter

1 cup sour cream

⅓ cup vegetable oil

2 eggs

1 cup sugar

1 teaspoon vanilla extract

2 cups flour

2 teaspoons baking powder

½ teaspoon baking soda

Pinch of salt

Crisp Topping

1 cup Entenmann's Chocolate Chip

Cookies of any variety

2 tablespoons flour

¼ cup walnuts

1 tablespoon sugar

½ teaspoon cinnamon

¼ teaspoon salt

3 tablespoons butter, softened

Directions

• Preheat oven to 350°F.

• Grease a 9x9-inch baking pan and line with parchment paper.

• Combine the sour cream with the oil, eggs, sugar, and vanilla. Set aside.

• In a separate bowl, stir together the flour, baking powder, baking soda, and salt.

• Fold the dry ingredients gently into the wet ones until combined. Mix well and pour into the prepared pan.

• In a processor, pulse the cookies until they are crumbs. Combine all the topping ingredients into a dry dough and sprinkle over the top of the pan.

• Bake for 40-45 minutes, until the cake has risen, the crumbs are golden, and a toothpick inserted into the cake come out clean.

• Remove from the pan and serve warm.

Cookie Milkshake

Serves 2

10 Entenmann's Chocolate Chip Cookies
of any variety

2 cups vanilla ice cream

1 teaspoon vanilla extract

1 cup whole milk

Directions

• Combine the milk and 8 of the Entenmann's Chocolate Chip Cookies in a cup, making sure the milk covers the cookies.

• Place the glass in the refrigerator and leave to soak for about 20 minutes.

• Drain the milk into a blender, leaving the cookies in the cup. Using a fork, mash up the cookies.

• Add the ice cream and the vanilla extract to the blender and process until smooth.

• Add the mashed cookies into the blender and blend for a few seconds to distribute.

• Pour the milkshake into two cold glasses and garnish with the remaining whole cookies. Serve with wide straws and spoons.

Caramel Breakfast Bake

Serves 8-10

1 Entenmann's All Butter Loaf cake, cut into slices about 1-inch thick

1 cup firmly packed light brown sugar

1 stick (½ cup) butter, softened

2 tablespoons light corn syrup

6 large eggs, beaten

1½ cups whole milk

1 teaspoon vanilla extract

Pinch of salt

Blackberries or other berries of choice to garnish

Directions

• Preheat oven to 350°F.

• Lightly grease a 13x9x2-inch baking dish.

• Combine the sugar, butter and corn syrup in a small pan and cook over a medium heat until thickened, stirring constantly.

• Line the baking dish with slices of loaf cake and cover the cake with the syrup mixture.

• In a large mixing bowl, combine the eggs, milk, vanilla extract and salt. Stir until blended. Pour the egg mixture over the cake.

• Cover and chill in the refrigerator for eight hours or overnight.

• Bake uncovered for 45 minutes or until lightly browned.

• Cut into slices and serve warm with each slice inverted so that the caramel is on top.

• Serve with berries.

You can use the Entenmann's Loaf Cake suggested or any of our classic selections or seasonal Loaf Cake favorites to make this recipe: All Butter, Marble, Chocolate Chip, Raisin, Sour Cream, Lemon, Cranberry Orange or Banana.

Easy Baklava

Serves 6-8

Cake

1 Entenmann's Sour Cream Loaf Cake

4 cups ground nuts (mixture of walnuts, almonds and pistachios)

½ cup sugar

2 teaspoons of ground cinnamon

Syrup

4 cups sugar

2 cups water

1 cinnamon stick

2 teaspoons lemon juice

Directions

- Slice the Entenmann's Sour Cream Loaf Cake in half horizontally.

- To make the filling, mix the ground nuts, sugar, and cinnamon in a bowl and stir together. Set the mixture aside.

- To make the syrup, in a saucepan, mix the sugar, water, and cinnamon stick. Boil for approximately 5 minutes, stirring, until the sugar is dissolved and the syrup has started to thicken.

- Stir in the lemon juice and remove from the heat. Take out the cinnamon stick.

- Cool for 15 minutes.

- Place one half of the cake on a platter. Spread with the nut mix filling. Top with the other half of the cake.

- Pour the syrup over the top and serve immediately.

You can use the Entenmann's Loaf Cake suggested or any of our classic selections or seasonal Loaf Cake favorites to make this recipe: All Butter, Marble, Chocolate Chip, Raisin, Sour Cream, Lemon, Cranberry Orange or Banana.

Cookie Truffles

Makes 18-20 truffles

One package Entenmann's Chocolate Chip
Cookies of any variety

¾ cup cream cheese, softened

1 cup semisweet chocolate pieces

Directions

- Put the cookies in a food processor and process until they are fine crumbs.

- Add the cream cheese to the crumbs and process until a sticky dough forms.

- Shape the dough into 1-inch round balls and place them on a greased baking sheet.

- Chill in the refrigerator for at least 2 hours, or preferably overnight.

- Melt the chocolate in short bursts in a microwave or in a glass dish over a pan of simmering water stirring constantly.

- Roll the chilled balls in the melted chocolate until they are completely coated, then carefully place on a wire rack.

- Set the rack on a baking sheet and chill in the refrigerator until the chocolate is completely set.

Raspberry & Chocolate Party Cups

Serves 4

1 Entenmann's Deluxe French Cheese Cake

1 cup dark chocolate pieces

¼ cup raspberry Jam

Pack fresh raspberries

2 tablespoons sliced almonds

Directions

• Melt the dark chocolate in a glass bowl over a pan of boiling water and add to the cupcake liners with a pastry brush or back of a small spoon. Place in the refrigerator to chill. When set, carefully peel away the liners and discard.

• To assemble, spread a teaspoon of jam in the bottom of each chocolate cup.

• Place a slice of Entenmann's Deluxe French Cheesecake into each of the cups.

• Slightly warm the remaining jam, and place a tablespoon on each of four dessert plates. This will help to hold the cups in place on the plate.

• Place the filled chocolate cups on top and garnish with fresh raspberries and almonds.

Little Bites Flying Saucers

Makes 15 pieces

1 box (15 brownies) Entenmann's Little
Bites Brownies

1 cup vanilla ice cream, softened

½ cup rainbow sprinkles or non pareils

Directions

• Cut each brownie in half horizontally.

• Take the vanilla ice cream out of the refrigerator 10-15 minutes before using it.

• Set a baking sheet in the freezer.

• Set up a cup of warm water. Scoop about 1 tablespoon of ice cream onto each bottom half of the brownies and smooth it with a spatula dipped in the warm water.

• Replace the top half of the brownie, pressing down firmly into the ice cream.

• Place the rainbow sprinkles or non pareils into a shallow dish and roll the prepared flying saucer into the mix until the ice cream is covered with sprinkles.

• Place the finished flying saucer immediately on a baking sheet in the freezer.

• Freeze for 2-3 hours and serve straight from the freezer.

Blueberries & Cream Crumb Bars

Serves 8-10

6 Entenmann's Glazed Buttermilk Donuts

1 tablespoon lemon zest

1 egg, beaten

½ cup natural almonds, ground

½ cup (1 stick) unsalted butter

2 cups fresh blueberries

2 tablespoons sugar

1 tablespoon fresh lemon juice

1½ tablespoons cornstarch

¼ cup marshmallow crème

½ tablespoon water

Directions

• Preheat oven to 350°F. Grease an 8x8 inch cake pan.

• Crumble the Entenmann's Glazed Buttermilk Donuts in a large bowl and set to one side.

• In a small bowl, mix the lemon zest, egg, almonds and butter. Add to the donut mixture. Press half of the mixture into the prepared cake pan. Bake for 8 minutes. Remove and let cool.

• In a pan, over medium heat, stir together the blueberries and sugar. Lightly mash the blueberries with a fork until syrupy.

• In a small cup, mix the lemon juice and cornstarch. Add to the blueberry mix, stirring over a low heat until the mixture thickens. Cool for 5 minutes before spreading over the donut crust.

• Heat the marshmallow crème in the microwave for 20 seconds. Stir in the water and whisk with a fork. Drizzle the marshmallow crème and water mixture over the blueberries. Top the bars with the remaining crumb mixture. Bake for 15 to 20 minutes, or until the crumb starts to brown.

• Let cool completely then refrigerate.

You can use the Entenmann's Donut variety suggested or any of our classic selections or seasonal favorites to make this recipe: Rich Frosted, Plain, Glazed, Crumb topped, Devil's Food, Cinnamon or Powdered.

A Pound of French Cake

Serves 4-6

1 Entenmann's Raisin Loaf Cake

3 large eggs

1 teaspoon cinnamon

1 can sliced peaches

6 tablespoons of butter pecan syrup

Directions

• Slice the Entenmann's Raisin Loaf Cake into 1-inch thick slices.

• Break the 3 eggs into a bowl and add 1 teaspoon of cinnamon. Beat together.

• Dip slices of the cake into the beaten egg mixture.

• Place on a griddle and cook on both sides until the egg mixture is well cooked and looks brown.

• Place the cooked slices onto a serving plate and pour the butter pecan syrup over the cake.

• Decorate with the peaches and serve.

*You can use the Entenmann's Loaf Cake suggested or any of our classic selections or seasonal Loaf Cake favorites to make this recipe: All Butter, Marble, Chocolate Chip, Raisin, Sour Cream, Lemon, Cranberry Orange or Banana.

Festive Loaf Cake

Serves 8-10

1 Entenmann's All Butter Loaf Cake

2 packets instant chocolate pudding mix

2 cups whipped topping, thawed or
marshmallow crème

Holiday sugars or sprinkles

Directions

• Prepare the instant chocolate pudding mix according
to the package instructions.

• Slice the Entenmann's All Butter Loaf Cake in
half horizontally and place the bottom half on a
serving plate.

• Spread half the pudding mixture over the cake.

• Place the top half of the loaf cake on top of the
pudding mix. Add the remaining pudding mix to the
top of the cake.

• Chill the cake for 2 hours in the refrigerator.

• Just before serving top with whipped topping or
marshmallow crème.

• Garnish with holiday sugars or sprinkles

• Cut into squares and serve immediately.

*You can use the Entenmann's Loaf Cake suggested or any of our classic selections or seasonal Loaf Cake favorites to make
this recipe: All Butter, Marble, Chocolate Chip, Raisin, Sour Cream, Lemon, Cranberry Orange or Banana.*

Banana Trifle Cake

Serves 8-10

1 Entenmann's All Butter or Sour Cream
Loaf Cake

2 packages instant banana pudding mix

2 tubs frozen whipped topping, thawed

2 cups milk chocolate chips.

Directions

• Slice the Entenmann's All Butter or Sour Cream Loaf Cake and then cut into small cubes.

• Prepare the banana pudding mix according to the package directions

• Layer a trifle bowl with the cake cubes covering the bottom of the bowl.

• Add just enough of the banana pudding mixture to cover the cake layer. Add in half of the whipped topping and a quarter cup of the chocolate chips.

• Add another layer of cake cubes and repeat the addition of a layer of banana pudding and layer of whipped topping.

• Chill in the refrigerator until ready to serve. Just before serving sprinkle with the remaining chocolate chips.

*You can use the Entenmann's Loaf Cake suggested or any of our classic selections or seasonal Loaf Cake favorites to make this recipe: All Butter, Marble, Chocolate Chip, Raisin, Sour Cream, Lemon, Cranberry Orange or Banana.

Café Caramel Tiramisu

Serves 4

2 Entenmann's Rich Frosted Donuts, sliced in half

1 cup brewed espresso

¼ cup sugar

2 cups whipping cream

1 cup mascarpone cheese

½ cup caramel topping, plus extra for drizzling

1 teaspoon dark chocolate syrup

1 can whipped cream

2 tablespoon semisweet chocolate shavings

Directions

• Stir the sugar into the brewed espresso in shallow bowl and refrigerate.

• Mix together the heavy cream and mascarpone cheese with an electric mixer until stiff peaks form.

• Add the caramel topping and chocolate syrup and beat until smooth.

• Break the Entenmann's Rich Frosted Donuts into halves and dip into the sweetened espresso. Shake off any excess liquid.

• To assemble, spoon ½ cup of heavy cream mixture into each of the four glasses or jars.

• Add 3 of the donut pieces on top of the cream mixture.

• Repeat with another layer and top with whipped cream, caramel drizzle, and chocolate shavings.

• Serve immediately

You can use the Entenmann's Donut variety suggested or any of our classic selections or seasonal favorites to make this recipe: Rich Frosted, Plain, Glazed, Crumb topped, Devil's Food, Cinnamon or Powdered.

Cookie Brownies

Makes 18-20 pieces

One package Entenmann's Chocolate Chip

Cookies of any variety

1 box of brownie mix

1 tablespoon of water

1 large egg, beaten

1 tub ready-made frosting (any flavor)

Directions

- Preheat oven to 350°F.

- Lightly grease a 13x9-inch baking pan.

- Prepare the brownie mix as directed on the instructions. Crumble in 1 pack of Entenmann's Chocolate Chip Cookies into the mix.

- Stir in 1 beaten egg and 1 tablespoon of water into the mixture.

- Pour the mixture into the prepared pan.

- Bake in the oven for 30 minutes. Remove from the oven and cool the brownies in the baking pan for 10 minutes.

- After 10 minutes remove from the pan onto a wire rack.

- Once cooled decorate the top with any flavor of frosting and cut into squares.

Meringue Cake

Serves 6-8

1 Entenmann's All Butter Loaf Cake

½ cup evaporated milk

½ cup sweetened condensed milk

½ cup heavy whipping cream

2 egg whites

3 tablespoons sugar

½ teaspoon vanilla extract

1 large ripe mango, peeled and sliced into "fingers" for garnish

Directions

• In a medium sized bowl mix the evaporated milk, sweetened condensed milk and whipping cream together with a spoon. Set aside.

• Place the Entenmann's All Butter Loaf Cake on a serving dish. With a long skewer or knife, poke holes all over the top of the Entenmann's All Butter Loaf Cake. Do not pierce the bottom of the cake

• Spoon the milk mixture over the Entenmann's All Butter Loaf Cake, trying to get the mixture down into the holes. When finished, cover with plastic wrap and refrigerate for at least 2 hours.

• About ½ hour before serving, place the egg whites in a medium size bowl. Using an electric mixer on high speed,

whip until soft peaks form. Lower speed to slow and gradually add the sugar and vanilla. Increase the speed to high and continue beating until stiff peaks form.

• Remove the cake from the refrigerator and remove plastic wrap. Using a spatula, spread the meringue over the entire cake making sure that it is at least half an inch thick. Decorate with swirls and peaks using the spatula evenly all around the cake.

• Using a kitchen torch, carefully brown the meringue being careful that it doesn't burn or place under the grill until browned.

• Arrange the mango pieces evenly around the cake on the serving dish and serve.

*You can use the Entenmann's Loaf Cake suggested or any of our classic selections or seasonal Loaf Cake favorites to make this recipe: All Butter, Marble, Chocolate Chip, Raisin, Sour Cream, Lemon, Cranberry Orange or Banana.

Strawberry Loaf Cake

Serves 6-8

1 Entenmann's All Butter Loaf Cake

1 tub of frozen whipped topping, thawed

2 cups fresh strawberries cut into quarters and slices.

Directions

• Slice the Entenmann's All Butter Loaf Cake in half horizontally.

• Hull and slice the strawberries.

• Spread a generous amount of the whipped topping onto one side of the loaf.

• Layer the sliced fresh strawberries onto the whipped topping.

• Assemble the layer cake and serve immediately.

*You can use the Entenmann's Loaf Cake suggested or any of our classic selections or seasonal Loaf Cake favorites to make this recipe: All Butter, Marble, Chocolate Chip, Raisin, Sour Cream, Lemon, Cranberry Orange or Banana.

Apple Cinnamon Swirl Bake

Serves 8-10

1 box Entenmann's Cinnamon Swirl Buns

1 medium baking apple (1-1½ cups),
peeled, cored and sliced

½ cup golden raisins

2 tablespoons sugar

½ teaspoon ground cinnamon

½ teaspoon nutmeg

5 eggs

1 cup whole milk

1 teaspoon vanilla extract

Directions

• Preheat the oven to 350°F.

• Grease a 13x9x2 inch cake pan.

• Slice the Entenmann's Cinnamon Swirl Buns into 1-inch thick slices and line the bottom of the baking dish.

• Combine the sugar and spices and sprinkle over the sliced apples. Place the apple slices and raisins on top of the buns. Top with the remaining bun slices.

• In a separate bowl beat together the eggs, milk and vanilla and pour over the bun mixture.

• Let set in the refrigerator overnight or for a minimum of 2 hours.

• Bake in the preheated oven for 40 minutes or until golden.

• Serve warm with maple syrup or cold with whipped cream and berries.

Cherry Fudge Cake

Serves 8-10

1 Entenmann's Chocolate Fudge Cake, refrigerated for a minimum of 4 hours

¼ cup of cherry brandy or maraschino cherry juice

1¼ cups frozen whipped topping, thawed

2 cups canned cherry pie filling

2 tablespoons semisweet chocolate shavings

Directions

- Remove the Entenmann's Chocolate Fudge Cake from the refrigerator and place on decorative serving platter.

- Using a fork, poke holes all over the surface deep into the cake layer.

- Slowly pour the cherry brandy or cherry juice over the cake allowing it to sink into holes. Set aside for one hour.

- Make a whipped cream border around inside edges of cake.

- Carefully spoon the cherry pie filling into the center.

- Place a dollop of whipped cream into the center and sprinkle with chocolate shavings.

- To make the chocolate sprinkles grate a chocolate bar with a cheese grater.

- Serve immediately.

*You can use the Entenmann's Iced Cake suggested or any of our classic selections or seasonal favorites to make this recipe: Chocolate Fudge, Thick Fudge Golden, Marshmallow Devil's Food, Carrot, Chocolate Chip or Vanilla Bean Iced cakes.

Berry Bruschetta Cake Stacks

Serves 4

1 Entenmann's All Butter Loaf Cake

4 tablespoons lemon curd

4 tablespoons blackberries

4 tablespoons orange marmalade

4 tablespoons raspberries

4 tablespoons whipped topping, thawed

4 teaspoons créme fraiche or sour cream

3 large strawberries, halved

Mint leaves for garnish

Directions

- Cut the Entenmann's All Butter Loaf Cake into 12 slices, then cut each slice into shapes of your choice (rounds, triangles, stars, etc.) making sure you have three of each shape.

- Grill the slices for 1-2 minutes or until lightly browned.

- To assemble, place 1 slice of cake on each of 4 dessert plates. Top with the lemon curd and blackberries.

- Place another slice on top of the blackberries and spread with marmalade and then top with the raspberries.

- Cover with a third slice of Entenmann's All Butter Loaf Cake.

- Combine the whipped topping and créme fraiche and place a dollop on top of the final slice.

- Garnish with mint leaves and serve immediately.

*You can use the Entenmann's Loaf Cake suggested or any of our classic selections or seasonal Loaf Cake favorites to make this recipe: All Butter, Marble, Chocolate Chip, Raisin, Sour Cream, Lemon, Cranberry Orange or Banana.

Chocolate Cherry Trifle

Serves 6-8

1 Entenmann's Sour Cream Loaf Cake

2 packets instant chocolate pudding mix made according to package directions

1 can cherry pie filling

1 cup almond slices

1 tub of frozen whipped topping, thawed

1 cup Maraschino cherries, chopped

Directions

- Cut the Entenmann's loaf cake into 1-inch cubes and place a third of the cubes into a large glass trifle bowl.

- Make the chocolate pudding mix according to the directions on the package.

- Add a third of the chocolate pudding mix on top of the loaf cake.

- Add a third of the whipped topping and sprinkle with a third of the almond slices.

- Finely chop two thirds of the Maraschino cherries and spinkle on top of the almond slices.

- Repeat the layering finishing with a final top layer of almonds.

- Refrigerate for 3 hours before serving, sprinkling with the remaning Maraschino cherries.

*You can use the Entenmann's Loaf Cake suggested or any of our classic selections or seasonal Loaf Cake favorites to make this recipe: All Butter, Marble, Chocolate Chip, Raisin, Sour Cream, Lemon, Cranberry Orange or Banana.

Fondue

Serves 4-6

1 Entenmann's All Butter Loaf Cake

6 cups semisweet chocolate chips

1½ cups heavy cream

Pinch of salt

½ cup dried apricots

½ cup fresh strawberries

1 cup marshmallows, pretzels and

other goodies to dip

Directions

•Combine the chocolate, heavy cream, and a pinch of salt in a glass dish.

•Set the glass dish over a pan of boiling water and melt over a low heat, stirring gently.

•Transfer to a fondue pot and keep the chocolate warm over a low heat.

•Slice and cube the Entenmann's All Butter Loaf Cake.

•Wash and prepare the fruit. Arrange the pound cake cubes and other fruits and dippables on a plate around the pot.

•Use fondue forks to dip cake cubes and other items into the chocolate.

•Serve with a side dish of whipped cream.

*You can use the Entenmann's Loaf Cake suggested or any of our classic selections or seasonal Loaf Cake favorites to make this recipe: All Butter, Marble, Chocolate Chip, Raisin, Sour Cream, Lemon, Cranberry Orange or Banana.

Stuffed French Crumb Cake

Serves 6-8

1 Entenmann's Butter French Crumb Cake

1 cup prepared vanilla pudding

1 cup frozen whipped topping, thawed

Directions

- Slice the Entenmann's Butter French Crumb Cake in half horizontally.

- Fold the vanilla pudding and whipped topping together and stir gently.

- Spread the pudding mixture over the bottom layer of the cake

- Carefully place the top layer with crumbs on top of the pudding mixture.

- Refrigerate until ready to serve.

*You can use the Entenmann's Crumb Cake variety suggested or any of our classic selections or seasonal Crumb Cake favorites to make this recipe.

Chocolate Peanut Butter Cups

Serves 4

1 Entenmann's Chocolate Fudge Cake

3 milk chocolate bars

⅓ cup creamy peanut butter

3 tablespoons confectioner's sugar

Peanuts, chopped, halved or whole for garnish

Directions

• Melt the chocolate bars, reserving 4 sections for garnish. Spoon the melted chocolate into 4 foil cupcake liners spreading the chocolate up the sides with a pastry brush or back of a small spoon. Place in the refrigerator to set. When chilled, carefully peel away the liners.

• In a small bowl, thoroughly combine the peanut butter and sugar and spread a tablespoon into the bottom of each chocolate cup.

• Slice the Entenmann's Chocolate Fudge Cake, place a slice into the bottom of each cup, pressing carefully to fit.

• Top each cup with remaining peanut butter mixture. Place a reserved section of the chocolate bar on top of each and sprinkle with peanuts.

*You can use the Entenmann's Iced Cake suggested or any of our classic selections or seasonal favorites to make this recipe: Chocolate Fudge, Thick Fudge Golden, Marshmallow Devil's Food, Carrot, Chocolate Chip or Vanilla Bean Iced cakes.

Coconut Cake with Spiced Berries

Serves 6-8

1 Entenmann's All Butter Loaf Cake

1 can sweetened condensed milk

1 teaspoon vanilla extract

1 teaspoon almond extract

¼ teaspoon ground cinnamon

3 cups shredded or flaked coconut

3 cups mixed frozen berries, defrosted

1 tablespoon sugar

2 teaspoons cornstarch

1 teaspoon candied ginger, chopped

¼ cup water

2 cups frozen whipped topping, thawed

Directions

• Preheat oven to 350°F.

• Grease a baking sheet.

• In a shallow 9-inch pie pan, combine the condensed milk, vanilla, almond extract, and cinnamon.

• Place the coconut onto a piece of waxed paper.

• Cut the Entenmann's All Butter Loaf Cake into 8 thick slices.

• To assemble, dip each slice into the condensed milk mixture, coating each side. Dip into coconut, coating all over. Place on the baking sheet and bake for 20 minutes or until golden brown. Set aside to cool.

• In a medium saucepan, place the defrosted berries. Mix with the sugar, cornstarch, ginger, and water and cook over medium heat until mixture comes to a boil and the sauce thickens, about 2 to 3 minutes.

• Serve the slices of coconut crusted cake topped with mixed berry compote and a side of whipped topping.

*You can use the Entenmann's Loaf Cake suggested or any of our classic selections or seasonal Loaf Cake favorites to make this recipe: All Butter, Marble, Chocolate Chip, Raisin, Sour Cream, Lemon, Cranberry Orange or Banana.

Donut Pudding with Zabaglione

Serves 8-10

16 Entenmann's Glazed Donuts, left out overnight to dry

½ cup (1 stick) unsalted butter

1 cup sugar

5 large eggs, lightly beaten

2 cups light cream

1 teaspoon ground cinnamon

1 tablespoon vanilla extract

2 tablespoons raisins

Zabaglione Sauce

3 cups vanilla ice cream

3 tablespoons Marsala wine

Directions

• Preheat oven to 350°F.

• Grease a 9x13-inch baking dish.

• In a food processor combine the butter and sugar. Add the eggs, cream, cinnamon, and vanilla, and process until blended.

• Break the donuts into 1-inch pieces and spread them in the prepared pan. Scatter the raisins over the top, and pour the egg mixture over all. Set aside to soak for 5 to 10 minutes, pushing the donut pieces down into the custard to ensure even coverage.

• Cover with foil and bake 35 to 40 minutes. Remove foil and bake for additional 10 minutes to brown the top. Donut pudding is done when the custard is set, but still soft.

• For zabaglione, microwave the ice cream for 20 seconds. Stir with a wooden spoon to loosen and then stir in Marsala wine.

• Cut the pudding into squares and serve topped with zabaglione.

You can use the Entenmann's Donut variety suggested or any of our classic selections or seasonal favorites to make this recipe: Rich Frosted, Plain, Glazed, Crumb topped, Devil's Food, Cinnamon or Powdered.

Lady Georgia Cake

Serves 6-8

1 Entenmann's All Butter Loaf Cake

2 cups peach slices

1 tablespoon sugar

½ pint vanilla ice cream, softened

6 tablespoons peach spread

½ cup pecans

2 cups freshly prepared whipped cream

Directions

• Place the sliced peaches in a bowl, sprinkle with sugar and mix together.

• Slice the Entenmann's All Butter Loaf Cake in half horizontally making two halves.

• Spread the bottom half with peach spread. Spread all the ice cream, half the peaches, and half the pecans over one of the halves.

• Gently place the other half on top.

• Frost the entire loaf with whipped cream and garnish with reserved peaches and pecans.

*You can use the Entenmann's Loaf Cake suggested or any of our classic selections or seasonal Loaf Cake favorites to make this recipe: All Butter, Marble, Chocolate Chip, Raisin, Sour Cream, Lemon, Cranberry Orange or Banana.

Muffin Pudding

Serves 8-10

1 Box Entenmann's Little Bites Chocolate
Chip Muffins, or any variety of Little Bites
Muffins

2 eggs, lightly beaten

½ cup firmly packed light brown sugar

½ cup sugar

2 cups heavy cream

½ cup evaporated milk

2 teaspoons vanilla extract

½ cup creamy peanut butter

Directions

• Preheat oven to 375°F.

• Lightly grease and flour a 9-inch dish.

• Cut each Entenmann's Little Bites Chocolate Chip Muffins into quarters and spread into the casserole dish.

• In a separate bowl, lightly beat the eggs. Add sugars and stir until combined. Add the heavy cream, evaporated milk and vanilla extract. Mix until well combined. Whisk in the peanut butter until smooth.

• Pour the mixture over the muffins, pressing the muffins down to ensure that each is soaked in liquid.

• Cook in a preheated oven for 45-60 minutes, or until the pudding is set and a toothpick comes out clean.

• Remove from oven, place on wire rack and let cool slightly.

• Serve at room temperature with chocolate fudge sauce, or warm with vanilla ice cream.

Fruit-tinis

Serves 4

1 package Entenmann's Little Bites
Brownies

1 package instant vanilla pudding

3 cups frozen whipped topping, thawed

3 cups fruit of your choice: bananas,
strawberries, raspberries, etc.

1 milk chocolate bar with almonds

2 tablespoons almond slices

Directions

• Prepare the instant vanilla pudding as directed on the
packet. Leave to cool.

• Take four martini glasses and break up two
Entenmann's Little Bites Brownies into each glass,
pressing them in to place.

• Add a half of cup of pudding to each glass. Then add two
layers of sliced bananas or strawberries.

• Add a scoop of whipped topping and smooth to the
edge of the glass.

• Finally, garnish with a sliced brownie bite, a piece of
fruit, and shave the chocolate bar over the top.

• Sprinkle with almonds and serve immediately.

Berry Cakes

Serves 8-10

4 Entenmann's Glazed Buttermilk Donuts
(or mixed Entenmann's Donuts)

1 cup fresh raspberries or strawberries

½ cup raspberry jam, warmed

2 cups frozen whipped topping, thawed

2 teaspoons confectioners' sugar

Directions

• Cut four Entenmann's donuts in half crosswise.

• Toss 1 cup whole raspberries or halved strawberries with ½ cup warm raspberry jam.

• Arrange berries on cut side of donuts, top with whipped topping.

• Garnish with confectioners' sugar.

*You can use the Entenmann's Donut variety suggested or any of our classic selections or seasonal favorites to make this recipe: Rich Frosted, Plain, Glazed, Crumb topped, Devil's Food, Cinnamon or Powdered.

Dreamy Chocolate Bars

Serves 10-12

1½ cups Entenmann's crumbled Rich Frosted Donuts (4 to 6 Donuts)

½ cup coarsely chopped caramel popcorn

1 large egg, lightly beaten

½ cup (1 stick) butter, melted

Topping

¼ cup firmly packed brown sugar

2 large eggs

1 cup hot fudge ice-cream topping

2 cups flaked coconut

1¼ cups dark chocolate chips

¾ cup semisweet chocolate chips

¾ cup cashew pieces

½ cup coarsely chopped caramel popcorn

Directions

- Preheat oven to 350°F.

- Lightly grease a 13x9x2-inch baking dish.

- For the crust, in a large bowl, combine the Entenmann's crumbled Rich Frosted Donuts, popcorn, egg, and butter.

- Press into the greased pan and bake for 12 to 15 minutes or until the edges are browned.

- Remove from the oven.

- For the topping, in a large mixing bowl, beat the sugar, egg and hot fudge topping, until blended. Fold in the remaining ingredients and pour the mixture over the crust.

- Bake for 25 - 35 minutes or until the edges are browned and the center is almost set.

- Cool on a wire rack before cutting into squares.

*You can use the Entenmann's Donut variety suggested or any of our classic selections or seasonal favorites to make this recipe: Rich Frosted, Plain, Glazed, Crumb topped, Devil's Food, Cinnamon or Powdered.

Almost Homemade **81**

Chocolate Chip Icebox Cake

Serves 8-10

2 packages Entenmann's Chocolate Chip
Cookies of any variety

½ cup confectioners' sugar

½ cup cream cheese

2½ cups heavy cream

Directions

• Grease a non-stick 9-inch round spring-form pan.

• Beat the cream cheese with the sugar until well combined and creamy.

• Add ½ cup heavy cream to the mixture and beat again. Add the remaining cream and beat until the mixture holds soft peaks.

• Arrange the cookies in the bottom of a the pan, breaking them as necessary to cover as much of the space as possible.

• Cover with one third of the cream, then arrange more cookies on top. Cover with more cream, another layer of cookies, with the last layer being a cream one.

• Wrap tightly with a plastic wrap and freeze overnight.

• Remove from the freezer and run a knife around the edges. Loosen from the pan and move the cake onto a serving plate.

• Serve immediately.

Brownie Cheesecake

Serves 8-10

1 Box Entenmann's Little Bites Brownies

3 large eggs

1 teaspoon vanilla extract

2 cups cream cheese, softened

⅓ cup sugar

Pinch salt

½ cup toasted pecans, chopped

1 teaspoon rum extract (optional)

Directions

• Pre-heat oven to 325°F. Grease an 8-inch springform pan with butter.

• Remove contents of 4 packs of Entenmann's Little Bites Brownies and crush with a rolling pin into crumbs.

• Press firmly into the bottom of the pan to form a crust.

• In a blender, or food processor place the eggs, vanilla extract, cream cheese, sugar and salt. Process until smooth and thoroughly combined. Pour over brownie the crust.

• Remove the remaining Entenmann's Little Bites Brownies from the packet and cut each brownie into 8 squares. Sprinkle on top of uncooked cheesecake, and gently press down below surface of cheese mixture.

• Bake for 45-50 minutes until the center is set, and edges appear brown.

• Cool for 15 minutes on wire rack.

• Refrigerate for 8 hours before serving.

I Love You Cake

Serves 8-10

1 Entenmann's Blackout Cake

1 cup semisweet chocolate, pieces

½ cup heavy cream

½ cup fresh raspberries

Mint leaves for decorating

Directions

• Using a 6-inch heart shaped cake pan as a template take a sharp knife and cut the Entenmann's Blackout cake into a heart shape.

• Prepare the frosting, place the chocolate and the heavy cream in a glass bowl in a saucepan of simmering water.

• Melt over a low heat stirring constantly.

• Carefully add the frosting to the top and sides of the cake with a spatula.

• Decorate with fresh raspberries and mint leaves.

*You can use the Entenmann's Iced Cake suggested or any of our classic selections or seasonal favorites to make this recipe: Chocolate Fudge, Thick Fudge Golden, Marshmallow Devil's Food, Carrot, Chocolate Chip or Vanilla Bean Iced cakes.

Quick & Easy Birthday Cake

Serves 8-10

1 Entenmann's Vanilla Bean Iced Cake

1 pack ready to use fondant

Chocolate candies for decorating

Candles for decorating

Directions

• Remove the Entenmann's Vanilla Bean Iced Cake from the tray and place on a decorative serving plate.

• Prepare the ready to use fondant outlined on the instructions.

• Roll the fondant into a square and lay gently on top of the Entenmann's Vanilla Bean Iced Cake. Trim base with a sharp knife.

• Decorate with chocolate candies and candles.

*You can use the Entenmann's Iced Cake suggested or any of our classic selections or seasonal favorites to make this recipe: Chocolate Fudge, Thick Fudge Golden, Marshmallow Devil's Food, Carrot, Chocolate Chip or Vanilla Bean Iced cakes.

Donuts, Danish & Puffs

Simple Donuts

Makes 10-12 Donuts

Batter

1 cup whole milk

4 packages (9 teaspoons) active dry yeast

2 cups all-purpose flour

2 tablespoons sugar

½ teaspoon salt

3 egg yolks

1 teaspoon vanilla extract

4 tablespoons butter, softened

Vegetable oil for greasing baking sheet and frying

Glaze (optional)

1½ cups confectioners' sugar

3–4 tablespoons water (or whole milk)

Directions

• Heat the milk until lukewarm and dissolve the yeast into the milk. Add 1½ cups of the flour into the mixture and set aside for 30 minutes.

• In a stand mixer fitted with a paddle attachment add the sugar, salt, egg yolks and vanilla and mix on low until smooth. Add the butter and milk and mix slowly.

• Change the paddle attachment to a dough hook and add the remaining flour. Mix slowly until the dough is smooth. Refrigerate the mixture for 60 minutes.

• Roll the dough onto a floured surface. The dough should be about ½ inch thick. Using a donut cutter cut out the donuts.

• Place on a greased baking sheet, cover with plastic wrap and leave in a warm place. The donuts should rise to nearly double the original size and spring back when touched.

• Heat 3 inches of vegetable oil in a heavy bottomed pan. The oil should be 360°F in temperature.

• Carefully place the donuts one at a time into the hot oil. Fry for 2 minutes or until golden brown. Remove with a slotted spoon and drain on a wire rack.

• To make the glaze, place the sugar in a bowl and slowly mix in the water or milk until smooth. Pour over the cooled donuts.

Double Chocolate Swirls

Makes 24 swirls

Batter

4½ cups white bread flour

1 package (2¼ teaspoons) active dry yeast

½ cup sugar

½ teaspoon salt

1 teaspoon ground cinnamon

6 tablespoons butter, softened

2 large eggs, beaten

1¼ cups whole milk

Filling and Glaze

6 tablespoons chocolate hazelnut spread

1 cup milk chocolate pieces

1 egg beaten

Directions

• Preheat the oven to 425°F.

• Lightly grease two baking sheets.

• Mix together the flour, yeast, sugar, salt, and cinnamon in a large bowl.

• Melt the butter in a heatproof bowl set over a saucepan of gently simmering water, then let cool slightly. Whisk in the eggs and milk. Pour into the flour mixture and mix well to form a dough.

• Turn out onto a floured surface and knead for 10 minutes, until smooth. Put into a large floured bowl, cover with plastic wrap, and put in a warm place for 1½–2 hours until double in bulk.

• Remove the dough from the bowl and punch down.

• Divide the dough into four pieces and roll each piece into a rectangle about 1 inch thick. Spread each rectangle with the chocolate hazelnut spread and scatter with the chopped chocolate.

• Roll up each rectangle from one of the long edges, then cut into six pieces. Place each swirl, cut-side down, on the prepared baking sheets and brush well with the beaten egg. Bake in the preheated oven for 12–15 minutes and serve warm.

Jelly Donuts

Makes 10 Donuts

Batter

Vegetable oil, for greasing and frying

3¼ cups white bread flour

4 tablespoons butter, cut into pieces

2 tablespoons sugar

½ teaspoon salt

1 package (2¼ teaspoons) active dry yeast

1 egg, lightly beaten

¾ cup lukewarm whole milk

Filling

½ cup seedless strawberry or raspberry jelly

Directions

• Lightly grease a large bowl and 2 baking sheets.

• Place the flour in a large bowl, add the butter, and rub it in until the mixture resembles breadcrumbs. Stir in the sugar, salt, and yeast. Make a well in the center and add the egg and milk, then mix to form a soft, pliable dough. Knead well for 10 minutes.

• Place in the greased bowl and cover. Leave in a warm place to rise for about 1 hour or until double in bulk.

• Knead the dough on a floured work surface, then divide into 10 pieces. Shape each piece into a ball and place on the baking sheets. Cover and leave in a warm place to double in size for 45 minutes.

• Heat 3-4 inches of oil in a saucepan to 360°F and deep-fry the donuts in batches for 2–3 minutes on each side. Drain on a paper towel and dust with sugar.

• To fill the donuts place the jam in a pastry bag fitted with a plain tip. Insert a sharp knife into each donut and twist to make a hole. Push the point of the tip into the hole and pipe in some jam.

Fruit Turnovers

Makes 8 turnovers

Pastry

1 pound puff pastry, thawed if frozen

All-purpose flour

1 egg for glazing

1 tablespoon water

Filling

4 tablespoons sugar

1 cup heavy cream or whipping cream

1 teaspoon vanilla extract

¼ cup raspberry or strawberry preserves

Directions

• Preheat the oven to 425°F.

• Line a large baking sheet with parchment paper.

• Roll the pastry out on a lightly floured work surface to a little larger than 10 inches square. Using a sharp knife, Trim the edges and cut out four 5-inch squares. Cut each square in half diagonally to produce 8 triangles and place on the lined baking sheet.

• Beat the egg with the water and brush over the tops of the triangles, being careful not to let it run down the sides. Sprinkle the tops with half the sugar.

• Bake in the preheated oven for 15 minutes, or until risen, crisp, and golden. Transfer to a wire rack to cool completely.

• Place the cream, remaining sugar, and vanilla extract in a large bowl and whip until peaks form. Spoon into a pastry bag fitted with a star tip. Split the puff pastry triangles in half horizontally and spread preserves on the bottom halves.

• Pipe the cream on top of the preserves and sandwich the 2 halves back together. Chill in the refrigerator until required.

Cream Éclairs

Makes 6-8 eclairs

Choux Pastry

⅔ cup water

5 tablespoons butter, cut into pieces

¾ cup all-purpose flour, sifted

2 eggs

Pastry Cream

2 eggs, lightly beaten

¼ cup sugar

2 tablespoons cornstarch

1¼ cups milk

¼ teaspoon vanilla extract

2 cups whipping cream

Frosting

2 tablespoons butter

1 tablespoon milk

1 tablespoon unsweetened cocoa

½ cup confectioners' sugar

¼ cup white chocolate pieces

Directions

- Preheat the oven to 400°F and lightly grease a baking sheet.

- To make the pastry, place the water in a saucepan, add the butter, and heat gently until the butter melts. Bring to a rolling boil, then remove the pan from the heat and add the flour all at once, beating well until the mixture leaves the sides of the pan and forms a ball. Let cool slightly, then gradually beat in the eggs to form a smooth, glossy mixture. Spoon into a large pastry bag fitted with a ½-inch plain tip.

- Sprinkle the baking sheet with water. Pipe éclairs 3- inches long, spaced apart. Bake in the oven for 30–35 minutes, until crisp and golden. Make a small slit in the side of each éclair to let the steam escape. Cool on a wire rack.

- Meanwhile, make the pastry cream. Whisk the eggs and sugar until thick and creamy, then fold in the cornstarch. Heat the milk in a saucepan until almost boiling and pour onto the egg mixture, whisking. Transfer the egg mixture to the saucepan and cook over low heat, stirring until thick. Remove the pan from the heat and stir in the vanilla extract. Cover with parchment paper and let cool. Once cool add in the 2 cups of whipped whipping cream.

- To make the frosting, melt the butter with the milk in a saucepan, remove from the heat, and stir in the cocoa and confectioners' sugar. Split the éclairs lengthwise and pipe in the pastry cream. Spread the frosting over the top of the éclairs. Melt a little white chocolate in a heatproof bowl set over a saucepan of simmering water, then spoon over the chocolate frosting and let set.

Sour Cream Donuts

Makes 24 Donuts

Batter

1 cup sugar

3 eggs

1 cup sour cream

1 teaspoon vanilla extract

2 tablespoons vegetable oil

3½ cups all-purpose flour

1 teaspoon baking soda

1 teaspoon baking powder

½ teaspoon salt

¼ teaspoon nutmeg

Vegetable oil for frying

Glaze

1½ cups confectioners' sugar

3-4 tablespoons water (or whole milk)

Directions

- In a large bowl beat sugar and eggs thoroughly. Add the sour cream and vanilla extract. Mix well.

- Add the dry ingredients and mix well again. Turn onto floured board and knead for 5 minutes. The dough should be fairly soft.

- Roll out the dough to ¼ inch thickness. Cut with a floured donut cutter.

- In a saucepan heat 3 inches of vegetable oil to 360°F. Cook the donuts in batches by dropping into the hot oil. Fry for 2 minutes or until golden brown.

- Remove with a slotted spoon and drain on a paper towel or wire rack.

- To make the glaze, place the sugar in a bowl and slowly mix in the water or milk until smooth.

- Pour the glaze over the cooled donuts.

Cinnamon Swirl Rolls

Makes 8 rolls

Batter

2½ cups self-rising flour

Pinch of salt

2 tablespoons sugar

1 teaspoon ground cinnamon

½ cup (1 stick) butter, melted

2 egg yolks

1 cup milk, plus extra for glazing

Filling

1 teaspoon ground cinnamon

¼ cup firmly packed light brown sugar

2 tablespoons sugar

1 tablespoon butter, melted

Frosting

1 cup confectioners' sugar, sifted

2 tablespoons cream cheese, softened

1 tablespoon butter, softened

2 tablespoons boiling water

1 teaspoon vanilla extract

Directions

- Preheat the oven to 350°F.

- Grease a baking sheet and line the bottom with parchment paper.

- Mix the flour, salt, sugar, and cinnamon together in a bowl. Whisk the butter, egg yolks, and milk together and combine with the dry ingredients to make a soft dough. Turn out onto a large piece of wax paper lightly sprinkled with flour, and roll out to a rectangle measuring 12x10 inches.

- To make the filling, mix the ingredients together, spread evenly over the dough, and roll up to form a log. Using a sharp knife, cut the dough into 8 even-size slices and pack into the prepared pan.

- Brush gently with extra milk and bake in the oven for 30–35 minutes, or until golden brown. Remove from the oven and let cool for 5 minutes before removing from the pan.

- To make the frosting, sift the confectioners' sugar into a large bowl and make a well in the center. Place the cream cheese and butter in the center, pour over the water, and stir to mix. Add extra boiling water, a few drops at a time, until the frosting coats the back of a spoon. Stir in the vanilla extract.

- Drizzle over the rolls. Serve warm or cooled.

Chocolate Cake Donuts

Makes 10-14 Donuts

Batter

½ cup whole milk (warmed)

1 egg

1 teaspoon vanilla extract

⅓ cup cocoa powder

1¾ cups all-purpose flour

½ teaspoon baking powder

½ teaspoon baking soda

½ teaspoon salt

½ cup sugar

2 tablespoons of butter

Vegetable oil for greasing baking sheet and frying

Glaze

¼ cup dark chocolate pieces

¼ cup white chocolate pieces

Directions

- In a bowl, blend together the warmed milk, egg and vanilla extract.

- In a mixer set up with a paddle attachment, mix the cocoa powder, flour, baking soda, baking powder, salt and sugar. Add the butter and blend. Slowly add the milk, egg and vanilla. Mix until the batter is smooth and thick and resembles cookie dough.

- Leave the dough to rest in the mixer for 20 minutes.

- Roll the dough onto a floured surface. The dough should be ½-inch thick. Using a donut cutter to cut out the donuts.

- Heat at least 3-inches of vegetable oil in a heavy bottomed pan. The oil should be 360°F. Carefully place the donuts one at a time into the oil. Fry for 2 minutes on each side or until golden brown. Remove with a slotted spoon and drain on a wire rack.

- To make the glaze, melt each of the chocolates separately over a pan of water. Coat the donuts making a pattern.

Cream Puffs

Makes 12 Puffs

Batter

¾ cup all-purpose flour

2 tablespoons unsweetened cocoa

Pinch of salt

6 tablespoons butter

I cup water

2 eggs, plus I egg white, beaten

Filling and Topping

2 teaspoons powdered gelatin

2 tablespoons water

3 cups strawberries, hulled

I cup ricotta cheese

I tablespoon sugar

2 teaspoons strawberry-flavored liqueur

Confectioners' sugar, for dusting

Directions

• Preheat the oven to 425°F. Line a baking sheet with parchment paper.

• To make the filling, sprinkle the gelatin over the water in a heatproof bowl. Let it soften for 2–3 minutes. Place the bowl over a saucepan of gently simmering water and stir until the gelatin dissolves. Remove from the heat.

• Place I cup of the strawberries in a blender with the ricotta cheese, sugar, and liqueur. Process until blended. Add the gelatin and process briefly. Transfer the mousse to a bowl, cover with plastic wrap, and chill for I–I½ hours, until set.

• To make the cream puffs, sift together the flour, cocoa, and salt. Put the butter and water into a heavy-bottom saucepan and heat gently until the butter has melted.

• Remove the pan from the heat and add the flour, cocoa, and salt all at once, stirring well until the mixture forms a paste and leaves the sides of the pan. Let cool slightly.

• Gradually beat the eggs and egg white into the flour paste and continue beating until it is smooth and glossy. Drop 12 rounded tablespoonfuls of the mixture onto the prepared baking sheet and bake in the preheated oven for 20–25 minutes, until puffed up and crisp. Remove from the oven and make a slit in the side of each puff. Return to the oven for 5 minutes. Transfer to a wire rack.

• Slice the remaining strawberries. Cut the petits choux in half, divide the mousse and strawberry slices among them, then replace the tops. Dust lightly with confectioners' sugar and place in the refrigerator. Serve within I½ hours.

Spiced Donut Holes

Makes 18-20 holes

Batter

½ cup whole milk (warm)

1 egg

2 tablespoons plain yogurt

1 teaspoon vanilla extract

1¾ cups all-purpose flour

2 teaspoons baking powder

½ teaspoon salt

⅓ cup sugar

1 teaspoon grated nutmeg

2 tablespoons butter

Vegetable oil for greasing baking sheet
and frying

Directions

• In a bowl blend together the warm milk, egg, yogurt and vanilla extract.

• In a mixer fitted with a paddle attachment mix the flour, baking powder, salt, sugar and nutmeg. Slowly add the butter and blend. Slowly add the milk mixture until the batter is smooth and thick and resembles cookie dough.

• Leave the dough to rest in the mixer for 20 minutes.

• Heat at least 3 inches vegetable oil in a heavy saucepan to 360°F.

• Drop dough 1 tablespoon at a time into the oil. Fry for one minute or until golden brown. Remove and drain on a paper towel or wire rack.

• Sprinkle with sugar and serve.

Crumb Cakes

Cinnamon Crumb Cake

Serves 9-12

Cake Batter

2½ cups all-purpose flour

1 teaspoon baking soda

¾ teaspoon baking powder

½ teaspoon salt

¾ cup (1½ sticks) unsalted butter

1½ cups sugar

2 large eggs

1½ cups sour cream

2 teaspoons vanilla extract

Topping

1 cup firmly packed light brown sugar

½ cup sugar

2 tablespoons ground cinnamon

1 tablespoon ground nutmeg

½ teaspoon salt

1 cup (2 sticks) unsalted butter

2½ cups all-purpose flour

Directions

• Preheat the oven to 350°F.

• Butter a 13x9x2-inch glass baking dish.

• To make the cake batter, sift the flour, baking soda, baking powder, and salt into a medium bowl.

• Using an electric mixer, beat the butter in large bowl until smooth. Add the sugar and beat until light and fluffy. Add eggs, 1 at a time, beating until well blended. Add sour cream and vanilla extract and beat until blended. Add flour mixture in 3 additions, beating until incorporated after each addition.

• Transfer the cake batter to prepared baking dish and spread evenly with spatula.

• To make the topping, mix both sugars, cinnamon, nutmeg and salt in medium bowl. Add warm melted butter and stir. Add flour and toss with fork until moist clumps form (topping mixture will look slightly wet).

• Squeeze small handfuls of topping together to form small clumps. Drop the topping clumps evenly over the cake batter, covering completely.

• Bake the cake for 45-50 minutes until toothpick inserted into center comes out clean and topping is deep golden brown and slightly crisp. Cool in the dish for at least 30 minutes before removing.

• Cut cake into squares and serve slightly warm or at room temperature.

Cream Cheese Swirl Coffee Cake

Serves 9-12

Cream Cheese Mix

1 cup cream cheese

2 tablespoons confectioners' sugar

1½ tablespoons lemon juice

Cake Batter

2 cups all-purpose flour

1 teaspoon baking powder

1 teaspoon baking soda

1 pinch salt

1 cup sugar

½ cup (1 stick) butter, softened

3 eggs, room temperature

2 teaspoons vanilla extract

1 cup sour cream

Topping

¼ cup finely chopped walnuts

2 tablespoons sugar

½ teaspoon cinnamon

½ teaspoon nutmeg

Directions

• Preheat oven to 350°F.

• Grease and flour a 9 cup Bundt pan.

• To make the cream cheese mix: in a small bowl, beat cream cheese, confectioners' sugar and lemon juice until smooth; set aside.

• To make the cake batter, stir together flour, baking powder, baking soda and salt. Set aside.

• In a large mixer bowl, beat the sugar and butter until fluffy. Add the eggs and vanilla mixing well. Add dry ingredients alternately with sour cream. Mix well.

• Pour half of batter into the pan. Spoon the cream cheese mixture on top of batter within ½ inch of pan edge. Spoon the remaining batter over the filling, spreading to the pan edge.

• To make the topping combine the chopped walnuts, sugar, ground cinnamon, and nutmeg. Sprinkle over the batter.

• Bake for 40–45 minutes or until a toothpick inserted near the center comes out clean. Cool for 10 minutes before removing from the pan. Serve warm.

Apricot Crumble Cake

Serves 9-12

Cake Batter

2 cups all-purpose flour

1 teaspoon baking powder

1 teaspoon baking soda

¾ teaspoon salt

½ cup (1 stick) unsalted butter, softened

1 cup sugar

1 teaspoon vanilla extract

2 large eggs

1 cup well-shaken buttermilk

Topping

2 cups flaked coconut

⅔ cup firmly packed light brown sugar

1 teaspoon cinnamon

⅓ cup melted butter

4 tablespoons apricot preserve

Filling

4 tablespoons apricot jam for filling

Directions

• Preheat the oven to 350°F.

• Line the bottom of a 9x2-inch round cake pan with parchment paper and butter the paper.

• To make the cake batter, sift together the flour, baking powder, baking soda, and salt. Beat together the butter and sugar in a large bowl with an electric mixer until pale and fluffy, then beat in the vanilla extract.

• Add eggs 1 at a time, beating well after each addition, then, with mixer at low speed, beat in all of buttermilk until just combined. Add flour mixture in 3 batches, mixing after each addition until just combined. Spoon batter into the cake pan, and bake for 45-50 until golden and a toothpick inserted in the middle comes out clean.

• Cool in the pan for 10 minutes before removing. Invert onto rack, then slide cake onto a cake plate. Slice the cake in half horizontally and spread with apricot preserve.

• For the topping, combine the coconut, brown sugar, cinnamon melted butter and apricot preserve. Mix well. Spread onto the cake and broil for 3–5 minutes until golden brown.

Pumpkin Crumb Cake

Serves 8-10

Cake Batter

1¾ cups all-purpose flour

1½ teaspoons pumpkin pie spice

1 teaspoon baking soda

1 teaspoon baking powder

¾ teaspoon salt

½ cup (1 stick) unsalted butter

1¼ cups sugar

3 large eggs

1 cup canned pureed pumpkin

1 teaspoon vanilla extract

⅓ cup milk

¾ cup chopped walnuts (optional)

Topping

⅔ cup plus 2 tablespoons rolled oats

½ cup all-purpose flour

½ cup firmly packed light brown sugar

½ teaspoon cinnamon

6 tablespoons unsalted butter

Directions

• Preheat oven to 350°F.

• Grease a 9x5x3-inch loaf pan and line with parchment paper.

• To make the topping, combine ⅔ cup oats, flour, sugar, and cinnamon in processor. Add butter and cut in until crumbly. Transfer mixture to medium bowl. Stir in remaining 2 tablespoons oats. Set to one side.

• Sift the flour, pumpkin spice, baking soda, baking powder, and salt into a bowl.

• In a separate bowl, beat the butter with an electric mixer until smooth. Gradually beat in the sugar and 1 egg at a time.

• Add the pumpkin and vanilla extract to the wet batter mix.

• Gradually beat the dry ingredients into the batter. Slowly add the milk and stir in the walnuts (optional). Transfer the batter to the prepared pan and spread with the topping.

• Bake the loaf cake until a toothpick inserted into center comes out clean, about 55 minutes. Cool in the pan for 15 minutes.

• Turn the cake out onto a rack and cool completely.

Blueberry Crumb Cake

Serves 9-12

Cake Batter

2 cups all-purpose flour

1 cup sugar

2 teaspoons baking powder

¾ teaspoon baking soda

1 teaspoon salt

1½ teaspoons cinnamon

1 teaspoon nutmeg

¾ cup (1½ sticks) unsalted butter

2 large eggs, lightly beaten

1 cup sour cream

¼ cup milk

2 teaspoons vanilla extract

2 tablespoons lemon extract

3 cups fresh blueberries

Topping

2 tablespoons sugar

2 tablespoons unsalted butter

1 cup all-purpose flour

Directions

• Preheat oven to 375°F.

• Butter a 13x9x2-inch baking pan and line with parchment paper.

• Whisk together flour, sugar, baking powder, baking soda, salt, cinnamon and nutmeg and put to one side.

• Blend butter into the flour with fingertips or a pastry blender until the mixture resembles a fine crumb.

• Whisk together the eggs, sour cream, milk, vanilla and add the flour mixture, stirring until combined.

• Fold the blueberries and lemon zest into the batter before adding the mix to the baking pan.

• To make the crumb topping, blend 2 tablespoons of butter with 1 cup of all purpose flour until the mixture resembles crumbs. Add two tablespoons sugar. Sprinkle over the batter mix.

• Bake until the cake is golden, or when tested a toothpick comes out clean. Generally 40 to 50 minutes. Cool the cake in pan for 20 minutes before serving.

Muffins

Lemon Poppy Seed Muffins

Makes 12 muffins

Muffin Batter

2 cups all-purpose flour

½ teaspoon salt

1½ teaspoons baking powder

¼ teaspoon baking soda

½ cup (1 stick) unsalted butter, softened

1 cup sugar

Finely grated zest from 2 lemons

2 large eggs

2 tablespoons lemon juice

1 cup sour cream

2 tablespoons poppy seeds

Glaze

1 tablespoon lemon juice

3 tablespoons confectioners' sugar

Directions

- Preheat oven to 350°F.

- Grease a 12 cup muffin pan or line with 12 paper baking cups.

- Whisk together the flour, salt, baking powder, and baking soda in a bowl, and set aside.

- In a mixing bowl, beat the butter, sugar, and lemon zest, until light and creamy. Beat in the eggs one at a time, mixing thoroughly. Stir in a third of the flour mixture until just combined. Stir in the lemon juice, and half of the sour cream until combined.

- Fold in half of the remaining flour mixture, and stir

until combined. Stir in the remaining sour cream. Finally stir in the remaining flour and poppy seeds.

- Fill the cups with batter. Bake for 20-25 minutes, or until golden brown and a toothpick inserted in the center comes out clean.

- While the muffins are baking make the glaze. Mix the lemon juice and powdered sugar together to form a thin glaze.

- Remove the muffins from the oven and cool for 5 minutes. Brush the lemon glaze evenly over the top of each muffin. When cool enough to handle, remove muffins from the cups and cool completely on a rack before serving.

Blueberry Muffin Supreme

Makes 12 muffins

Muffin Batter

3 cups all-purpose flour

¾ teaspoon salt

1 tablespoon baking powder

½ teaspoon baking soda

1 cup sugar

½ cup (1 stick) butter, softened

Finely grated zest from one lemon

2 tablespoons vegetable oil

2 large eggs

1 cup sour cream

½ cup whole milk

½ teaspoon lemon extract, optional

2 cups fresh blueberries

Directions

• Preheat oven to 375°F.

• Grease a 12 cup muffin pan or line with 12 paper baking cups.

• Sift together the flour, salt, baking powder, and baking soda into a bowl. Set aside.

• In a large mixing bowl, beat the sugar, butter, lemon zest, and vegetable oil until light and creamy. Beat in the eggs one at a time. Whisk in the sour cream, milk, and lemon extract.

• Add half the flour mixture and stir until combined. Fold in the rest of the flour and mix thoroughly.

• Fold in the blueberries with a spatula until just combined.

• Fill each cup with batter and bake for 25-30 minutes until golden brown.

• When cool, remove muffins from the cups and serve.

Double Chocolate Chip Muffins

Makes 8 muffins

Muffin Batter

½ cup (1 stick) butter, softened

½ cup sugar

2 large eggs

¾ cup self-rising flour

½ cup semisweet chocolate chips

½ cup cocoa powder

Directions

- Preheat the oven to 375°F.

- Grease 8 cup muffin pan or line with 8 paper baking cups.

- In a bowl, sift together the flour, and cocoa powder. Set aside.

- In a large mixing bowl beat together the butter, sugar and eggs until smooth.

- Add half the dry ingredients and stir until combined. Add the remaining dry ingredients. Fold in the chocolate chips until combined.

- Spoon the batter into the prepared muffin cups.

- Bake in the preheated oven for 20–25 minutes, or until well risen and springy to the touch.

- Transfer to a wire rack and leave to cool.

Orange & Cranberry Muffins

Makes 12 muffins

Muffin Batter

1½ cups dried cranberries

3 tablespoons fresh orange juice

2 cups all-purpose flour

1 tablespoon baking powder

Pinch of salt

½ cup sugar

2 large eggs

1 cup whole milk

6 tablespoons vegetable oil

Finely grated rind of 1 orange

Directions

- Preheat the oven to 400°F.

- Grease a 12 cup muffin pan or line with 12 paper baking cups.

- Put the cranberries in a bowl, add the orange juice, and let soak for 1 hour.

- Sift together the flour, baking powder, and salt into a large bowl. Stir in the sugar.

- Lightly beat the eggs in a large bowl, then beat in the milk, oil, and orange rind. Make a well in the center of the dry ingredients, pour in the beaten liquid ingredients, and add the soaked cranberries. Stir gently until just combined; do not overmix.

- Spoon the batter into the prepared muffin cups. Bake in the preheated oven for about 20 minutes, until well risen, golden brown, and firm to the touch.

- Let the muffins cool in the pan for 5 minutes, then serve warm or transfer to a wire rack and let cool completely.

Chocolate Marshmallow Muffins

Makes 12 muffins

Muffin Batter

1 cup mini white marshmallows

1½ cups all-purpose flour

½ cup unsweetened cocoa

1 tablespoon baking powder

Pinch salt

½ cup firmly packed light brown sugar

2 large eggs

1 cup whole milk

6 tablespoons vegetable oil

Directions

• Preheat the oven to 400°F.

• Grease a 12 cup muffin pan or line with 12 paper baking cups.

• Using scissors, cut the marshmallows in half.

• Sift together the flour, cocoa, baking powder, and salt into a large bowl. Stir in the sugar and marshmallows.

• Lightly beat the eggs in a large bowl, then beat in the milk and oil.

• Make a well in the center of the dry ingredients and pour in the beaten liquid ingredients. Stir gently until just combined. Do not overmix.

• Spoon the batter into the muffin pan. Bake in the preheated oven for about 20 minutes, until well risen and firm to the touch.

• Let the muffins cool in the pan for 5 minutes, then serve warm or transfer to a wire rack and let cool completely.

Jelly Donut Muffins

Makes 12 muffins

Muffin Batter

2 cups all-purpose flour

1 tablespoon baking powder

Pinch of salt

½ cup sugar

2 large eggs

1 cup whole milk

6 tablespoons vegetable oil

1 teaspoon vanilla extract

4 tablespoons strawberry or raspberry jelly

Topping

½ cup butter

¾ cup sugar

Directions

- Preheat the oven to 400°F.

- Grease a 12 cup muffin pan or line with 12 paper baking cups.

- Sift together the flour, baking powder, and salt into a large bowl. Stir in the sugar.

- Lightly beat the eggs in a large bowl, then beat in the milk, oil, and vanilla extract. Make a well in the center of the dry ingredients and pour in the beaten liquid ingredients. Stir gently until combined.

- Spoon half the batter into the muffin cups. Add a teaspoon of jelly to the center of each then spoon in the remaining batter.

- Bake in the preheated oven for about 20 minutes, until well risen, golden brown, and firm to the touch.

- To make the topping, melt the butter. Spread the sugar in a wide, shallow bowl. When the muffins are baked, let them cool for 5 minutes. Dip the tops of the muffins in the melted butter then roll in the sugar.

- Serve warm or transfer to a wire rack and let cool completely.

Banana Muffins

Makes 12 muffins

Muffin Batter

⅓ cup raisins

3 tablespoons fresh orange juice

1 cup all-purpose flour

1 cup self-rising whole wheat flour

1 tablespoon baking powder

½ cup sugar

2 bananas, mashed

½ cup whole milk

2 large eggs

6 tablespoons vegetable oil

Grated rind of 1 orange

Directions

• Preheat the oven to 400°F.

• Grease a 12 cup muffin pan or line with 12 paper baking cups.

• Put the raisins in a bowl, add the orange juice, and let soak for 1 hour.

• Sift together both types of flour and the baking powder into a large bowl. Stir in the sugar.

• In a bowl, whisk the mashed bananas and the milk into a puree.

• Lightly beat the eggs in a large bowl, then beat in the banana and milk mixture, oil, soaked raisins, and orange rind. Make a well in the center of the dry ingredients and pour in the beaten liquid ingredients. Stir gently until just combined, do not overmix.

• Spoon the batter into the muffin cups. Bake in the preheated oven for about 20 minutes, until well risen, golden brown, and firm to the touch.

• Let the muffins cool in the pan for 5 minutes, then serve warm or transfer to a wire rack and let cool completely.

Carrot Cake Muffins

Makes 12 muffins

Muffin Batter

2 cups all-purpose flour

1 tablespoon baking powder

Pinch of salt

1 teaspoon apple pie spice

½ cup firmly packed light brown sugar

1 cup grated carrots

½ cup chopped walnuts or pecans

½ cup golden raisins

2 large eggs

¾ cup whole milk

6 tablespoons vegetable oil

Finely grated rind and juice of 1 orange

Strips of orange zest, to decorate

Frosting

½ cup soft cream cheese

3 tablespoons butter

⅓ cup confectioners' sugar

Directions

• Preheat the oven to 400°F.

• Grease a 12 cup muffin pan or line with 12 paper baking cups.

• Sift together the flour, baking powder, salt, and apple pie spice into a large bowl. Stir in the sugar, grated carrots, walnuts, and golden raisins.

• Lightly beat the eggs in a large bowl, then beat in the milk, oil, orange rind, and orange juice. Make a well in the center of the dry ingredients and pour in the beaten liquid ingredients. Stir gently until just combined; do not overmix.

• Spoon the batter into the muffin pan. Bake in the preheated oven for about 20 minutes, until well risen, golden brown, and firm to the touch.

• Let the muffins cool for 5 minutes, then transfer to a wire rack and let cool completely.

• To make the frosting, put the cream cheese and butter in a bowl and sift in the confectioners' sugar. Beat together until light and fluffy. When the muffins are cold, spread the frosting on top of each, then decorate with strips of orange zest.

• Chill the muffins in the refrigerator until ready to serve.

Spicy Apple Muffins

Makes 12 muffins

Muffin Batter

1 cup all-purpose flour

1 tablespoon baking powder

1 teaspoon apple pie spice

½ cup firmly packed light brown sugar

2 cups rolled oats

2 large baking apples (2 cups), chopped and diced

2 large eggs

½ cup whole milk

½ cup unsweetened apple juice

6 tablespoons vegetable oil

Directions

• Preheat the oven to 400°F.

• Grease a 12 cup muffin pan or line with 12 paper baking cups.

• Sift together the flour, baking powder and apple pie spice into a large bowl. Stir in the sugar and 1 cup of the oats.

• Finely chop the unpeeled apples, discarding the cores. Add to the flour mixture and stir together.

• Lightly beat the eggs in a large bowl, then beat in the milk, apple juice, and oil. Make a well in the center

of the dry ingredients and pour in the beaten liquid ingredients. Stir gently until just combined; do not overmix.

• Spoon the batter into the muffin cups. Sprinkle the tops of the muffins with the remaining oats. Bake in the preheated oven for about 20 minutes, until well risen, golden brown, and firm to the touch.

• Let the muffins cool in the pan for 5 minutes, then serve warm or transfer to a wire rack and let cool completely.

Frosted Cream Cheese Muffins

Makes 12 muffins

Muffin Batter

½ cup soft cream cheese

½ cup sugar

2 cups all-purpose flour

1 tablespoon baking powder

Pinch of salt

½ cup firmly packed light brown sugar

2 large eggs

1 cup sour cream

6 tablespoons vegetable oil

Finely grated rind of lemon

2 teaspoons fresh lemon juice

Frosting

½ cup soft cream cheese

⅓ cup confectioners' sugar

2 teaspoons fresh lemon juice

Directions

• Preheat the oven to 400°F.

• Grease a 12 cup muffin pan or line with 12 paper baking cups.

• Put ½ cup of the cream cheese in a bowl. Sift in 1 tablespoon of the confectioners' sugar and beat together.

• Sift together the flour, baking powder, and salt into a large bowl. Stir in the brown sugar.

• Lightly beat the eggs in a large bowl, then beat in the sour cream, oil, and lemon rind. Make a well in the center of the dry ingredients and pour in the liquid ingredients. Stir gently until combined, do not overmix.

• Spoon half the batter into the muffin cups. Add a spoonful of the cream cheese mixture to the center of each, then spoon in the remaining batter. Bake in the preheated oven for about 20 minutes, until well risen, golden brown, and firm to the touch.

• Let the muffins cool for 5 minutes, then transfer to a wire rack and let cool completely.

• To make the frosting, put the cream cheese in a bowl and sift in the confectioners' sugar. Add the lemon juice and beat well together. Spread the frosting on top of the muffins. Chill in the refrigerator until ready to serve.

Raspberry Crumble Muffins

Makes 12 muffins

Muffin Batter

2 cups all-purpose flour

1 tablespoon baking powder

½ teaspoon baking soda

Pinch of salt

½ cup sugar

2 large eggs

1 cup plain yogurt

6 tablespoons vegetable oil

1 teaspoon vanilla extract

1 cup frozen raspberries

Topping

½ cup all-purpose flour

3 tablespoons butter

2 tablespoons sugar

Directions

- Preheat the oven to 400°F.

- Grease a 12 cup muffin pan or line with 12 paper baking cups.

- To make the topping, put the flour into a bowl. Cut the butter into small pieces, add to the bowl with the flour, and rub it in with your fingertips until the mixture resembles fine breadcrumbs. Stir in the sugar and set aside.

- To make the muffins, sift together the flour, baking powder, baking soda, and salt into a large bowl. Stir in the sugar.

- Lightly beat the eggs in a large bowl, then beat in the yogurt, oil, and vanilla extract. Make a well in the center of the dry ingredients, pour in the beaten liquid ingredients, and add the raspberries. Stir gently until just combined, do not overmix.

- Spoon the batter into the muffin cups. Scatter the crumble topping over each muffin and press down lightly. Bake in the preheated oven for about 20 minutes, until well risen, golden brown, and firm to the touch.

- Let the muffins cool in the pan for 5 minutes, then serve warm or transfer to a wire rack and let cool completely.

Sour Cream Muffins

Makes 12 muffins

Muffin Batter

2 cups all-purpose flour

Pinch of salt

1 tablespoon baking powder

½ cup sugar

2 large eggs

1 cup sour cream

6 tablespoons vegetable oil

1 teaspoon vanilla extract

Directions

• Preheat oven to 375°F.

• Grease a 12 cup muffin pan or line with 12 paper baking cups.

• Sift together the flour, salt, baking powder and sugar into a bowl. Set aside.

• In a large mixing bowl lightly beat the eggs. Then beat in the sour cream, oil, and vanilla extract.

• Add half the flour mixture and stir until combined. Fold in the rest of the flour and mix thoroughly.

• Fill each cup with batter and bake for 20-25 minutes until golden brown.

• When cool, remove muffins from the cups and serve.

Loaf Cakes

Lemon Loaf Cake

Serves 8-10

Batter

1½ cups all-purpose flour

1 tablespoon baking powder

¾ cup (1½ sticks) butter, softened

¾ cup sugar

3 eggs, beaten

1 egg yolk

Finely grated rind of 1 lemon

2 tablespoons lemon juice

Fine strips of lemon zest, to decorate

Syrup

¾ cup confectioners' sugar

3 tablespoons lemon juice

Directions

- Preheat the oven to 350°F.

- Grease a 9x5x3-inch loaf pan and line with parchment paper.

- Sift the flour and baking powder into a large bowl and add the butter, sugar, eggs, and egg yolk. Beat well until the mixture is smooth, then stir in the lemon rind and juice.

- Spoon the mixture into the prepared pan and smooth the surface with a spatula. Bake in the preheated oven for 40–50 minutes, or until well risen and golden brown.

- Remove the pan from the oven and transfer to a wire rack.

- For the syrup, put the confectioners' sugar and lemon juice into a pan and heat gently without boiling, stirring, until the sugar dissolves.

- Prick the top of the loaf several times with a toothpick and spoon the syrup over it. Let cool completely in the pan, then turn out, sprinkle with strips of lemon zest, and serve in slices.

Loaf Cake with Orange Glaze

Serves 8-10

Batter

2 cups all-purpose flour

1 teaspoon baking powder

¼ teaspoon baking soda

½ teaspoon salt

1 cup (2 sticks) unsalted butter

1¼ cups sugar

1 tablespoon grated lemon zest

1 tablespoon grated orange zest

4 eggs

½ cup buttermilk

1 teaspoon vanilla extract

Glaze

1 cup confectioners' sugar

1½ tablespoons fresh orange juice

1 tablespoon freshly grated orange zest

Directions

• Preheat oven to 325°F.

• Grease a 9x5x3-inch loaf pan and line with parchment paper.

• Sift together the flour, baking powder, baking soda, and salt in a mixing bowl.

• In a large mixing bowl, using an electric mixer beat the butter, sugar, and zests until light and creamy. Beat in the eggs, one at time, beating very thoroughly after each addition.

• Using a spatula mix in the flour alternately with the buttermilk, ending with flour.

• Scrape the batter into the prepared loaf pan.

• Bake for 60 minutes, or until a toothpick inserted in the center comes out clean. Remove and let rest for 15 minutes, then turn onto a cooling rack. Let cool for 15 more minutes before glazing.

• To make the glaze. In a bowl, combine the sugar and orange juice, adding enough orange juice to get a smooth spreadable consistency. Apply to the top of the warm cake.

• Let the loaf cake cool completely before serving.

Banana Loaf Cake

Serves 8-10

Batter

1 cup white self-rising flour

¾ cup whole wheat flour

¾ cup firmly packed light brown sugar

Pinch of salt

½ teaspoon ground cinnamon

½ teaspoon ground nutmeg

2 large ripe bananas, mashed

¾ cup orange juice

2 eggs, beaten

4 tablespoons vegetable oil

Directions

• Preheat the oven to 350°F.

• Grease a 9x5x3-inch loaf pan and line with parchment paper.

• Sift the flours, sugar, salt, and the spices into a large bowl. Set aside.

• In a separate bowl, mash the bananas with the orange juice, then beat in the eggs and oil. Pour into the dry ingredients and mix well.

• Spoon the batter into the prepared loaf pan and bake in the preheated oven for 60 minutes or until a toothpick inserted into the center comes out clean.

• Remove from the oven and let cool in the pan. Turn out the loaf, slice, and serve.

Banana & Cranberry Loaf Cake

Serves 8-10

Batter

1½ cups self-rising flour

½ teaspoon baking powder

1 cup firmly packed light brown sugar

2 bananas, mashed

¼ cup chopped orange and lemon peel

⅓ cup chopped mixed nuts

⅓ cup dried cranberries

5–6 tablespoons orange juice

2 eggs, beaten

⅔ cup vegetable oil

Frosting

⅔ cup confectioners' sugar, sifted

2 teaspoons water

Grated rind of 1 orange

Directions

• Preheat the oven to 350°F.

• Grease a 9x5x3-inch loaf pan and line with parchment paper.

• Sift the flour and baking powder into a large mixing bowl. Stir in the brown sugar, bananas, mixed peel, nuts, and cranberries.

• Stir together the orange juice, eggs, and oil until well combined, then add the mixture to the dry ingredients and mix until well blended. Pour into the prepared pan.

• Bake in the preheated oven for about 60 minutes, until firm to the touch and a toothpick inserted into the center comes out clean.

• Turn out onto a wire rack and let cool.

• Mix the confectioners' sugar with a little water and drizzle the frosting over the loaf. Sprinkle the orange rind over the top. Let the frosting set before slicing.

Blackberry & Apple Loaf Cake

Serves 8-10

Batter

2 large apples (2 cups) peeled and diced

3 tablespoons lemon juice

2½ cups self-rising whole wheat flour

½ teaspoon baking powder

1 teaspoon ground cinnamon

½ cup blackberries, thawed, if frozen

¾ cup firmly packed brown sugar

1 egg, beaten

1 cup low-fat plain yogurt

Topping

14 white or brown sugar cubes, crushed

¼ cup blackberries, thawed, if frozen

Directions

• Preheat the oven to 375°F.

• Grease a 9x5x3-inch loaf pan and line with parchment paper.

• Peel, core, and finely dice the apples. Place them in a saucepan with the lemon juice, bring to a boil, cover, and simmer for about 10 minutes, until soft and pulpy. Beat well and set aside to cool.

• Sift the flour, baking powder, and cinnamon into a bowl. Stir in ½ cup of the blackberries and the sugar.

• Make a well in the center of the ingredients and add the egg, yogurt, and cooled apple puree. Mix well to incorporate thoroughly.

• Spoon the batter into the prepared pan and smooth the top. Sprinkle with the remaining blackberries, pressing them down into the cake batter, and top with the crushed sugar lumps. Bake in the preheated oven for 40–45 minutes. Remove from the oven and set aside in the pan to cool.

• Serve dusted with cinnamon.

Chocolate Chip Loaf Cake

Serves 8-10

Batter

3¼ cups all-purpose flour

1 teaspoon salt

2 cups (4 sticks) unsalted butter

2 cups sugar

1½ teaspoons vanilla extract

8 large eggs, lightly beaten

2 cups semisweet chocolate chips

Glaze

1 cup semisweet chocolate chips

5 tablespoons coffee liqueur

1 tablespoon vanilla extract

1 tablespoon light corn syrup

Directions

- Preheat the oven to 350°F.

- Grease two 9x5x3-inch loaf pans and line with parchment paper.

- Combine the flour and salt in a bowl and set aside.

- With an electric mixer, cream the butter and sugar until pale and fluffy. Stir in the vanilla extract.

- In a large bowl, lightly beat the 8 eggs and add to the butter and sugar mix. Fold in the flour and mix thoroughly. Fold the semisweet chocolate chips into the finished batter. Divide the batter between the pans.

- Bake until a toothpick inserted into center of each cake comes out clean, about 65 minutes. Let cool in pans on a wire rack for 30 minutes before removing from the pans.

- To make glaze, heat the chocolate chips, coffee liquer, vanilla extract and light corn syrup in a glass bowl set in a simmering pan of water. Whisk until smooth.

- Pour over cake and for a special treat serve with whipped cream.

Pound Cake Loaf

Serves 8-10

Batter

3¼ cups all-purpose flour

1 teaspoon salt

1 tablespoon baking powder

2 cups (4 sticks) unsalted butter

2 cups sugar

1½ teaspoons vanilla extract

8 large eggs

Directions

• Preheat oven to 350°F.

• Grease two 9x5x3-inch loaf pans and line with parchment paper.

• Combine the flour, baking powder and the salt in a bowl and set aside.

• In a large bowl, cream the butter and sugar with a mixer until pale and fluffy. Add the vanilla extract and mix thoroughly.

• Lightly beat 8 large, room-temperature eggs and add to the butter and sugar. Mixing until just incorporated. Fold in the flour. Divide the batter between pans.

• Bake until a toothpick inserted into center of each cake comes out clean, about 65 minutes.

• Cool pans on a wire rack for 30 minutes before removing the cakes from the pans.

• Dust with a sprinkling of sugar.

Blueberry Sour Cream Loaf Cake

Serves 8-10

Batter

3¼ cups all-purpose flour

1 teaspoon salt

1½ cups (3 sticks) unsalted butter

½ cup sour cream

2 cups sugar

1½ teaspoons vanilla extract

8 large eggs

2 cups of blueberries

2 tablespoons all-pupose flour

2 tablespoons sugar for sprinkling onto prepared batter

Glaze

1 cup heavy cream

1 tablespoon confectioners' sugar

2 teaspoons lemon zest

Directions

• Preheat the oven to 350°F.

• Grease two 9x5x3-inch loaf pans and line with parchment paper.

• Combine the flour and salt in a bowl and set aside.

• With an electric mixer, cream butter, sour cream, and sugar on high speed until pale and fluffy. Add the vanilla extract.

• Lightly beat 8 eggs and add to the creamed butter mixture. Mix in the flour until incorporated. Toss the blueberries in the 2 tablespoons of flour before adding to the batter.

• Divide the batter between the pans. Sprinkle 2 tablespoons of sugar over each cake.

• Bake until a toothpick inserted into center of each cake comes out clean, about 65 minutes.

• Cool on a wire rack for 30 minutes before removing the cakes from the pans.

• To make the glaze mix together the cream, sugar, and lemon zest. Spread on the cake or serve on the side.

Poppy Seed Loaf Cake

Serves 8-10

Batter

3¼ cups all-purpose flour

1 teaspoon salt

2 cups (4 sticks) unsalted butter

2 cups sugar

1½ teaspoons vanilla extract

8 large eggs

1 tablespoon poppy seeds

Directions

• Preheat oven to 350°F.

• Grease two 9x5x3-inch loaf pans and line with parchment paper.

• Combine the flour and salt into a bowl and set aside.

• Cream the butter and sugar with an electric mixer on high speed until pale and fluffy. Add the vanilla extract.

• Lightly beat the 8 eggs and add to the creamed butter and sugar. Fold in the flour and the poppy seeds. Mix thoroughly. Divide the batter between the pans.

• Bake in the oven until a toothpick inserted into center of each cake comes out clean, about 65 minutes.

• Cool in pans on a wire rack for 30 minutes before removing.

• Sprinkle with additional poppy seeds before serving.

Date & Walnut Loaf Cake

Serves 8-10

Batter

½ cup chopped pitted dates

½ teaspoon baking soda

Finely grated rind of ½ lemon

½ cup hot black tea

3 tablespoons butter

⅓ cup firmly packed light brown sugar

1 egg

1 cup self-rising flour

¼ cup chopped walnuts

Walnut halves, to decorate

Directions

• Preheat the oven to 350°F.

• Grease a 9x5x3-inch loaf pan and line with parchment paper.

• Place the dates, baking soda, and lemon rind in a bowl and add the hot tea. Let soak for 10 minutes, until softened.

• Cream together the butter and sugar until light and fluffy, then beat in the egg. Stir in the date mixture.

• Fold in the flour using a large metal spoon, then fold in the chopped walnuts. Spoon the mixture into the prepared loaf pan and spread evenly. Top with walnut halves.

• Bake in the preheated oven for 35–40 minutes, or until risen, firm, and golden brown. Cool for 10 minutes in the pan, then turn out the loaf and finish cooling on a wire rack.

Chocolate Peanut Butter Loaf Cake

Serves 8-10

Batter

2¼ cups all-purpose flour

1 cup unsweetened cocoa powder

1 teaspoon salt

2 cups (4 sticks) of unsalted butter

2 cups of sugar

8 large eggs

1½ teaspoons vanilla extract

2 cups semi-sweet chocolate chips

Glaze

4 tablespoons peanut butter

5 tablespoons whole milk

Directions

• Preheat oven to 350°F.

• Grease two 9x5x3-inch loaf pans and line with parchment paper.

• Combine the flour, cocoa powder and salt in a bowl and set aside.

• Cream the butter and sugar with an electric mixer on high speed until pale and fluffy. Add the vanilla extract.

• Lightly beat 8 eggs and add to the butter and sugar mix, mixing until just incorporated. Fold the chocolate chips into the batter.

• Divide the batter between the pans. Bake until a test inserted into center of each cake comes out clean, about 65 minutes.

• Cool in pans on a wire rack for 30 minutes before removing.

• To make the glaze combine the peanut butter and 5 tablespoons of milk and wisk until smooth. Add more milk if necessary to achieve the desired consistency. Drizzle over the cooled loaf.

Chocolate & Orange Loaf Cake

Serves 8-10

Batter

½ cup semisweet chocolate pieces

⅔ cup (1½ sticks) butter, softened

1¼ cups sugar

5 large eggs, beaten

1 cup all-purpose flour

2 teaspoons baking powder

Pinch of salt

Grated rind of 2 oranges

Directions

• Preheat the oven to 350°F.

• Grease two 9x5x3-inch pans and line with parchment paper.

• Place the chocolate in a bowl set over a pan of simmering water, making sure that the bottom of the bowl does not touch the water. Remove from the heat once the chocolate has melted.

• Place the butter and sugar in a separate bowl and cream with a mixer until light and fluffy. Gradually beat in the eggs. Sift the flour, baking powder, and salt into the mixture and fold in.

• Transfer one-third of the mixture to the melted chocolate and stir. Stir the orange rind into the remaining mixture and spread one-fourth of the mixture evenly in each cake pan.

• Drop spoonfuls of the chocolate mixture on top, dividing it between the pans, but do not smooth it out. Divide the remaining orange mixture between the pans, then, using a knife, gently swirl the top 2 layers together to give a marbled effect.

• Bake for 35–40 minutes, or until a toothpick inserted comes out clean. Let cool in the pans for 10 minutes before removing.

Cinnamon Raisin Loaf Cake

Serves 8-10

Batter

3¼ cups all-purpose flour

1 teaspoon salt

2 cups (4 sticks) unsalted butter

2 cups sugar

1½ teaspoon vanilla extract

8 large eggs

2 cups raisins

2 tablespoons cinnamon

2 tablespoons flour for raisins

Glaze (optional)

2 cups confectioners' sugar

4 tablespoons whole milk

Directions

• Preheat oven to 350°F.

• Grease two 9x5x3-inch loaf pans and line with parchment paper.

• Combine the flour and the salt in a bowl and set aside.

• Cream together the butter and sugar with a mixer on high speed until pale and fluffy. Add the vanilla extract.

• Lightly beat 8 eggs and add to the butter and sugar. Mix thoroughly and fold in the flour and salt, mixing until just incorporated.

• Toss the raisins in 2 tablespoons of flour and gently fold the raisins into the batter.

• Divide the batter in half, folding the cinnamon into 1 half. Add the batter to the pan, alternating the plain and cinnamon batter. Swirl together with a knife.

• Bake until a toothpick inserted into center of each cake comes out clean. About 65 minutes. Cool in pans for 30 minutes before removing.

• To make the glaze, combine the sugar and milk in a bowl. Add more milk if necessary to make the right consistency. Drizzle over the cooled cake.

Brown Sugar Walnut Loaf Cake

Serves 8-10

Batter

3¼ cups all-purpose flour

1 teaspoon salt

2 cups (4 sticks) unsalted butter

2 cups firmly packed light brown sugar

1½ teaspoon vanilla extract

8 large eggs

2 cups toasted chopped walnuts

Directions

- Preheat oven to 350°F.

- Grease two 9x5x3-inch loaf pans and line with parchment paper.

- Combine the flour and salt in a bowl and set aside.

- Cream the butter and brown sugar with an electric mixer on high speed until pale and fluffy. Add the vanilla extract and mix thoroughly.

- Lightly beat 8 eggs and add to the butter and sugar. Mix thoroughly. Fold in the flour and salt and mix well. Fold the chopped walnuts into the batter.

- Divide the batter between the pans.

- Bake until a toothpick inserted into center of each cake comes out clean, about 65 minutes. Cool in pans on a wire rack for 30 minutes before removing.

Marbled Loaf Cake

Serves 8-10

Batter

⅓ cup semisweet chocolate pieces

3 tablespoons whole milk

5 tablespoons butter

½ cup sugar

1 egg, beaten

3 tablespoons sour cream

1 cup self-rising flour

½ teaspoon baking powder

½ teaspoon vanilla extract

Directions

• Preheat the oven to 325°F.

• Grease a 9x5x3-inch loaf pan and line with parchment paper.

• Melt the chocolate, place it in a small heatproof bowl with the milk, and set the bowl over a saucepan of simmering water. Heat gently until just melted. Remove from the heat.

• Cream together the butter and sugar until light and fluffy. Beat in the egg and sour cream. Sift the flour and baking powder over the mixture, then fold in using a metal spoon.

• Spoon half the batter into a separate bowl and stir in the chocolate mixture. Add the vanilla extract to the plain batter.

• Spoon the chocolate and vanilla batters alternately into the prepared loaf pan, swirling lightly with a knife for a marbled effect. Bake for 40–45 minutes, or until well risen and a toothpick when inserted comes out clean.

• Cool in the pan for 10 minutes, then turn out and finish cooling on a wire rack.

Ginger Loaf Cake

Serves 8-10

Batter

1½ cups all-purpose flour

1 tablespoon baking powder

1 tablespoon ground ginger

¾ cup vegetable oil

½ cup dark brown sugar

⅓ cup corn syrup

3 eggs, beaten

3 pieces preserved ginger in syrup plus

2 tablespoons syrup from jar

Sliced preserved ginger to decorate

(available from specialty stores)

Directions

• Preheat oven to 350°F.

• Grease a 9x5x3-inch loaf pans and line with parchment paper.

• Combine the flour, baking powder and ground ginger into a large bowl. Add in the oil, corn syrup and eggs and then beat well to a smooth batter. Stir in the chopped ginger.

• Pour the mixture into the prepared pan. Bake in the preheated oven for 65 minutes or until a toothpick inserted into center of each cake comes out clean.

• Cool in the pan for 10 minutes then turn out onto a wire rack.

• To serve, brush the cake with the ginger syrup. Arrange the sliced ginger on top and cut into slices.

Brownies & Bars

Black & White Brownies

Makes 24 brownies

Cream cheese Mix

6 tablespoons (¾ stick) butter

I cup cream cheese

¾ cup sugar

3 eggs

3 tablespoons all-purpose flour

I tablespoon vanilla extract

Chocolate Mix

½ cup (I stick) butter

2 cups semisweet chocolate pieces

6 eggs

2¼ cups sugar

I½ cups all-purpose flour

I½ teaspoons baking powder

I½ teaspoons salt

I½ tablespoons vanilla extract

I teaspoon almond extract

Directions

• Preheat oven to 350°F.

• Grease a 13x9-inch baking pan.

• Prepare the chocolate mix. Slowly melt the chocolate and the butter in a glass bowl placed over a pan of gently simmering water. Mix well and set aside to cool.

• To make the cream cheese mix, cream the butter then add the cream cheese and sugar. Beat until fluffy and add in the eggs, then the flour, and vanilla extract.

• In a separate bowl complete the chocolate mix. Whip the eggs and sugar until fluffy. Stir together the flour, baking powder, salt, and mix into egg mixture. Mix in the melted chocolate and butter, and add the vanilla and almond extract.

• Spread half the chocolate mixture into the pan. Then spread with the cream cheese mixture. Spoon the remaining chocolate batter on top. Swirl the two mixtures together with a knife.

• Bake for 40 minutes. Cool and cut into bars.

Double Chocolate Brownies

Makes 16 brownies

Batter

½ cup (1 stick) butter

⅔ cup semisweet chocolate pieces

1⅓ cups sugar

Pinch of salt

1 teaspoon vanilla extract

2 eggs

1 cup all-purpose flour

2 tablespoons unsweetened cocoa

½ cup white chocolate chips

Fudge sauce

4 tablespoons (½ stick) butter

1 cup sugar

⅔ cup whole milk

1 cup heavy cream

⅔ cup dark corn syrup

1 cup semisweet chocolate pieces

Directions

• Preheat the oven to 350°F.

• Grease an 8-inch square cake pan and line the bottom with parchment paper.

• Place the butter and chocolate in a small heatproof bowl set over a saucepan of gently simmering water until melted. Stir until smooth. Let cool slightly. Stir in the sugar, salt, and vanilla extract. Add the eggs, one at a time, stirring well, until blended.

• Sift the flour and cocoa into the cake batter and beat until smooth. Stir in the chocolate chips, then pour the batter into the prepared pan.

• Bake in the preheated oven for 35–40 minutes, or until the top is evenly colored and a toothpick inserted into the center comes out almost clean. Let cool slightly while you prepare the sauce.

• To make the fudge sauce, place the butter, sugar, milk, cream, and corn syrup in a small saucepan and heat gently until the sugar has dissolved. Bring to a boil and stir for 10 minutes, or until the mixture is caramel-colored. Remove from the heat and add the chocolate. Stir until smooth. Cut the brownies into squares and serve immediately with the sauce.

Almond & Raspberry Bars

Makes 12 bars

Crust

1½ cups all-purpose flour

½ cup (1 stick) butter

2 tablespoons sugar

1 egg yolk

1 tablespoon cold water

Filling

½ cup (1 stick) butter

½ cup sugar

1 cup ground almonds

3 eggs, beaten

½ teaspoon almond extract

4 tablespoons raspberry preserve

2 tablespoons slivered almonds

Directions

• Preheat the oven to 400°F.

• Grease a 9-inch square cake pan.

• For the dough, sift the flour into a bowl and rub in the butter with your fingertips until the mixture resembles fine breadcrumbs. Stir in the sugar, then combine the egg yolk and water and stir in to make a firm dough, adding a little more water if necessary. Wrap in plastic wrap and chill in the refrigerator for about 15 minutes, until firm enough to roll out.

• Roll out the dough and line the cake pan. Prick the bottom and chill for 15 minutes.

• For the filling, cream the butter and sugar together until pale and fluffy, then beat in the ground almonds, eggs, and almond extract.

• Spread the preserve over the bottom of the crust, then top with the almond filling, spreading it evenly. Sprinkle with the slivered almonds.

• Bake in the preheated oven for 10 minutes, then reduce the temperature to 350°F and bake for an additional 25–30 minutes, or until the filling is golden brown and firm to the touch. Cool in the pan, then cut into bars.

Lemon Drizzle Bars

Makes 12 bars

Batter

2 eggs

¾ cup sugar

⅔ cup (1½ sticks) soft margarine

Finely grated rind of 1 lemon

1½ cups self-rising flour

½ cup whole milk

Syrup

1¼ cups confectioners' sugar

¼ cup fresh lemon juice

Confectioners' sugar, for dusting

Directions

• Preheat the oven to 350°F.

• Grease an 8-inch square cake pan and line with parchment paper.

• Place the eggs, sugar, and margarine in a bowl and beat hard until smooth and fluffy. Stir in the lemon rind, then fold in the flour lightly and evenly. Stir in the milk, mixing evenly, then spoon the batter into the prepared cake pan, smoothing level.

• Bake in the preheated oven for 45–50 minutes, or until golden brown and firm to the touch. Remove from the oven and place the pan on a wire rack.

• To make the syrup, place the confectioners' sugar and lemon juice in a small saucepan and heat gently, stirring until the sugar dissolves. Do not boil.

• Prick the warm cake all over with a skewer and spoon the hot syrup evenly over the top.

• Let cool completely in the pan, then turn out the cake, cut into 12 pieces, and dust with a little confectioners' sugar before serving.

Trail Mix Bar

Makes 16 bars

Batter

¾ cup (1½ sticks) margarine

3 tablespoons honey

¾ cup firmly packed light brown sugar

½ cup smooth peanut butter

3 cups rolled oats

¼ cup chopped dried apricots

2 tablespoons vegetable oil

2 tablespoons sesame seeds

Directions

• Preheat the oven to 350°F.

• Grease and line a 9-inch square baking pan with parchment paper.

• Melt the margarine, honey, and sugar in a saucepan over low heat. When the sugar has dissolved, add the peanut butter and stir until everything is well combined.

• Add the oats, apricots, vegetable oil and sesame seeds and mix well.

• Press the mixture into the prepared pan and bake in the preheated oven for 20 minutes or until golden brown.

• Remove from the oven and let cool in the pan, then cut into 16 squares and serve.

Cinnamon Raisin Bars

Makes 16 bars

Batter

½ cup (1 stick) butter

1 cup firmly packed light brown sugar

1½ cups all-purpose flour

1½ cups quick-cooking oats

½ teaspoon baking soda

½ teaspoon salt

2 tablespoons water

1 egg

Raisin Filling

¼ cup sugar

1 teaspoon cinnamon

1 tablespoon cornstarch

1 cup water

2 cups raisins

Directions

• Preheat the oven to 350°F.

• Grease a 13x9x2-inch baking pan.

• In a mixing bowl, cream together the butter and brown sugar. Set aside.

• In a separate bowl combine the flour, egg, oats, baking soda and salt. Add the mixture to the creamed butter and brown sugar mix. Stir together with the water and beat until crumbly.

• Press half the mixture into the baking pan and pat the mixture firmly into place with the back of a spoon.

• To make the filling, in a saucepan, combine the sugar, cinnamon, cornstarch and water and stir until smooth. Add the raisins. Cook the mixture over a medium heat until it is thick and bubbly.

• Cool to room temperature; spread over the crust. Top the filling with the remaining oat mixture and press down firmly.

• Bake for 30–35 minutes or until golden brown. Cool on a wire rack.

Chocolate Fudge Brownies

Makes 9 brownies

Batter

1¼ cups semisweet chocolate pieces

½ cup (1 stick) butter

1 cup sugar

Pinch of salt

2 tablespoons water

2 large eggs

1 teaspoon vanilla extract

¾ cup all-purpose flour

½ cup chopped walnuts (optional)

Directions

• Preheat oven to 325°F.

• Grease an 8-inch-square baking pan.

• Place the chocolate, butter, sugar, salt, and water in small saucepan over a very low flame. Heat, stirring often, until the chocolate and butter are melted and the sugar dissolved.

• Pour into a mixing bowl. Stir in the eggs, one at a time. Stir in the vanilla extract. Stir in the flour. Fold in the nuts, if using.

• Pour the batter into the prepared pan.

• Bake for 35 minutes. Cool completely before cutting into 9 squares.

• Dust with confectioners' sugar if desired.

Cranberry Sour Cream Brownies

Makes 12 brownies

Batter

½ cup (1 stick) butter

1 cup self-rising flour

4 tablespoons unsweetened cocoa

1 cup firmly packed dark brown sugar

2 eggs, lightly beaten

1¼ cups fresh cranberries

Topping

⅔ cup sour cream

1 tablespoon sugar

1 tablespoon self-rising flour

1 egg yolk

½ teaspoon vanilla extract

Directions

• Preheat the oven to 350°F.

• Grease and lightly flour a shallow 9x13-inch baking pan.

• Place the butter, cocoa, and sugar in a saucepan and stir over low heat until just melted. Let cool slightly. Quickly stir in the flour and eggs and beat hard until thoroughly mixed to a smooth batter. Stir in the cranberries.

• Spread the batter into the pan.

• To make the topping, place all the ingredients in a bowl and beat together until smooth. Spoon over the chocolate batter, swirling evenly with a spatula.

• Bake in the preheated oven for 35–40 minutes, or until risen and firm.

• Let cool in the pan, then cut into squares.

Apricot Bars

Makes 10 bars

Batter

¾ cup (1½ sticks) butter

½ cup firmly packed light brown sugar

¼ cup honey

¾ cup dried apricots, chopped

2 teaspoons sesame seeds

2⅔ cups rolled oats

Directions

• Preheat the oven to 350°F.

• Very lightly grease a shallow 11x7-inch rectangular baking pan.

• Place the butter, sugar, and honey in a small saucepan over low heat and heat until the ingredients have melted together.

• Stir in the apricots, sesame seeds, and oats. Spoon the mixture into the pan and lightly smooth the top.

• Bake in the preheated oven for 20–25 minutes, or until golden brown.

• Cut into 10 bars and let cool completely in the pan.

Nutty Granola Bars

Makes 16 bars

Batter

½ cup (1 stick) butter

2⅓ cups rolled oats

¾ cup chopped hazelnuts

½ cup all-purpose flour

2 tablespoons dark corn syrup

½ cup firmly packed light brown sugar

Directions

- Preheat the oven to 350°F.

- Grease a 9-inch square cake pan.

- Place the oats, hazelnuts, and flour in a large bowl and stir together.

- Place the butter, dark corn syrup, and sugar in a sauce-pan over low heat and stir until the butter has melted and the sugar is dissolved.

- Pour onto the dry ingredients and mix well.

- Spoon the mixture into the pan and smooth the top.

- Bake in the preheated oven for 20–25 minutes, or until golden and firm to the touch.

- Cut into 16 pieces and let cool in the pan until cold.

Chocolate Peppermint Bars

Makes 16 bars

Dough

4 tablespoons (½ stick) butter

¼ cup sugar

¾ cup all-purpose flour

Filling

1½ cups confectioners' sugar

1–2 tablespoons warm water

½ teaspoon peppermint extract (optional)

2 teaspoons green food coloring

Topping

1 cup semisweet chocolate pieces

Directions

• Preheat the oven to 350°F.

• Grease and line a 13x9-inch baking pan with parchment paper.

• Place the butter and sugar in a large bowl and beat together until light and fluffy. Stir in the flour until the mixture binds together.

• Knead the mixture to form a smooth dough, then press into the pan and prick the surface all over with a fork. Bake in the preheated oven for 10–15 minutes, or until lightly browned and just firm to the touch. Let cool in the pan.

• Sift the confectioners' sugar into a bowl. Gradually add the water, then add the peppermint extract and food coloring, if using. Spread the icing over the base, then let set.

• Place the chocolate in a heatproof bowl, set the bowl over a saucepan of gently simmering water, and heat until melted. Spread the chocolate over the icing, then let set in a refrigerator for at least one hour.

• Cut into bars and serve.

Sticky Pecan Pie Bars

Makes 10 bars

Crust

2 tablespoons butter

1¼ cups all-purpose flour

¼ cup firmly packed light brown sugar

Topping

2 large eggs

6 tablespoons melted butter

½ cup firmly packed light brown sugar

⅓ cup chopped pecans

½ cup dark corn syrup

½ teaspoon vanilla extract

Directions

• Preheat the oven to 375°F.

• Line a shallow 9-inch square baking pan with parchment paper and grease the paper.

• Place 2 tablespoons of the butter in a saucepan and heat gently until melted. Let cool slightly.

• Place the flour and remaining butter, cut into cubes, in a large bowl and rub the butter in with your fingertips until the mixture resembles fine breadcrumbs. Stir in ¼ cup of the sugar, then spoon the mixture into the pan and press down firmly with the back of a spoon. Bake in the preheated oven for 20 minutes.

• Meanwhile, place the eggs in a large bowl and beat lightly. Add the remaining sugar, the pecans, melted butter, dark corn syrup, and vanilla extract and stir together until combined.

• Pour the mixture over the crust in the pan and bake in the oven for an additional 15–20 minutes, or until firm to the touch and golden brown. Remove from the pan and let cool. When cold, cut into 10 bars to serve.

Apple & Cinnamon Bars

Makes 14 bars

Crust

½ cup (1 stick) unsalted butter

⅔ cup sugar

1 teaspoon vanilla extract

2 eggs, beaten

1 cup all-purpose flour

2 large baking apples (2 cups) peeled,
cored, and diced

2 tablespoons lemon juice

Topping

⅓ cup finely chopped, blanched almonds

¼ cup all-purpose flour

¼ cup firmly packed light brown sugar

½ teaspoon ground cinnamon

2 tablespoons unsalted butter, melted

Directions

• Preheat the oven to 350°F.

• Grease and line a 11x7-inch cake pan.

• Cream together the butter, sugar, and vanilla extract until pale. Gradually add the eggs, beating thoroughly. Sift in the flour and fold in evenly.

• Prepare the apples by peeling, dicing and sprinkling with lemon juice. Add to the flour mixture and mix.

• Spread the mixture into the bottom of the cake pan. Pat the mixture down with the back of a wooden spoon or spatula.

• For the topping, mix all the ingredients to a crumbly texture and sprinkle over the cake. Bake the cake in the preheated oven for 45–55 minutes, until firm and golden.

• Cut into bars and serve warm or cooled.

No-Bake Chocolate Fingers

Makes 14 bars

Cake Mix

1 cup semisweet chocolate pieces

4 tablespoons butter, softened

2 tablespoons dark corn syrup

1 cup graham cracker pieces

1¼ cups mixed dried fruit

¼ cup candied cherries

Directions

- Grease an 11x7-inch cake pan and line with parchment paper.

- Place the chocolate in a heatproof bowl, set the bowl over a saucepan of gently simmering water, and heat until melted.

- Add the butter and dark corn syrup and stir until combined. Remove from the heat.

- Stir the crackers into the chocolate along with the mixed fruit and cherries.

- Pour the chocolate mixture into the pan. pressing down well with the back of a spoon. Chill for 2 hours, or until firm.

- Cut into 14 fingers to serve.

Chocolate Oat Bars

Makes 16 bars

Oat Mix

1 cup all-purpose flour

1 cup quick cooking oats

¾ cup firmly packed light brown sugar

½ cup (1 stick) butter

Filling

½ teaspoon vanilla extract

1 can sweetened condensed milk

1 cup chopped nuts

1 cup semisweet chocolate chips

Directions

• Preheat oven to 350°F.

• Grease a 13x9-inch baking pan.

• In large bowl, combine the flour, oats, sugar and butter mixing them together well. Reserve ½ cup of the oat mixture. Press the remainder of the mixture into the bottom of the prepared pan.

• Bake for 10 minutes.

• Pour the sweetened condensed milk and vanilla over the baked crust. Sprinkle with the nuts and the chocolate chips.

• Top with the remaining oat mixture and press down firmly.

• Bake for 25–30 minutes or until lightly browned. Cool and cut into bars.

Marshmallow Crunch Bars

Makes 8 bars

Batter

1 ½ cups all-purpose flour

1 tablespoon baking powder

¾ cup (1½ sticks) unsalted butter, softened

¾ cup sugar

3 eggs beaten

1 teaspoon vanilla extract

½ cup chopped mixed nuts

⅓ cup candied cherries, chopped

½ cup mini marshmallows

Directions

- Preheat oven to 350°F.

- Grease a 9-inch square baking pan.

- In large bowl, combine the flour and baking powder and add the butter, sugar eggs and vanilla extract. Beat well until the mixture is smooth.

- Stir ⅔ of the nuts, marshmallows and chopped cherries into the mixture.

- Spoon into the prepared pan and smooth the top with a spatula.

- Bake in the oven for 40-50 minutes until risen and golden brown.

- Let cool in the pan for 20 minutes, until firm, then cut into bars and finish cooling on a wire rack.

Cookies

Peanut Butter Cookies

Makes about 26 cookies

Dough

½ cup (1 stick) butter, softened

½ cup crunchy peanut butter

½ cup sugar

½ cup firmly packed light brown sugar

1 egg, beaten

½ teaspoon vanilla extract

⅔ cup all-purpose flour

½ teaspoon baking soda

½ teaspoon baking powder

Pinch of salt

1½ cups rolled oats

Directions

• Preheat the oven to 350°F.

• Grease several baking sheets.

• Place the butter and peanut butter in a bowl and beat together. Beat in the sugar and brown sugar, then gradually beat in the egg and vanilla extract.

• Sift the flour, baking soda, baking powder, and salt into the bowl and stir in the oats.

• Place spoonfuls of the cookie dough onto the baking sheets, spaced well apart to allow for spreading. Flatten slightly with a fork.

• Bake in the preheated oven for 12 minutes, or until lightly browned.

• Let cool on the baking sheets for 2 minutes, then transfer to wire racks to cool completely.

Oatmeal, Raisin & Nut Cookies

Makes about 30 cookies

Dough

½ cup chopped raisins

½ cup orange juice

1 cup (2 sticks) butter, softened

¾ cup sugar

1 egg yolk, lightly beaten

2 teaspoons vanilla extract

2 cups all-purpose flour

Pinch of salt

½ cup rolled oats

½ cup chopped hazelnuts

Whole hazelnuts, to decorate

Directions

• Preheat the oven to 375°F.

• Line 2 baking sheets with parchment paper.

• Put the raisins in a bowl, add the orange juice, and let soak for 10 minutes.

• Put the butter and sugar into a large bowl and mix well with a wooden spoon, then beat in the egg yolk and vanilla extract. Sift the flour and salt into the mixture and add the oats and chopped hazelnuts. Drain the raisins, discarding the orange juice. Add them to the mixture, and stir until thoroughly combined.

• Drop tablespoons of the mixture onto the prepared baking sheets, spaced well apart. Flatten slightly and place a whole hazelnut in the center of each cookie.

• Bake in the preheated oven for 12–15 minutes, until golden brown. Let cool on the baking sheets for 5–10 minutes, then carefully transfer the cookies to wire racks to cool completely.

Vanilla Sugar Cookies

Makes about 12 cookies

Dough

1½ cups all-purpose flour

¾ cup (1½ sticks) butter cut into pieces

1 cup sugar

1 teaspoon vanilla extract

Directions

• Preheat the oven to 350°F.

• Grease several baking sheets.

• Sift the flour into a large bowl. Add the butter and rub it in with your fingertips until the mixture resembles fine breadcrumbs. Stir in the sugar and vanilla extract and mix together to form a firm dough.

• Roll out the dough on a lightly floured counter to a thickness of ½ inch. Stamp out 12 hearts with a heart-shaped cookie cutter. Arrange the hearts on the prepared baking sheet.

• Bake in the preheated oven for 15–20 minutes, or until just colored. Transfer to a wire rack and let cool completely.

• Dust with a little sugar just before serving.

Blueberry & Cranberry Cookies

Makes about 30 cookies

Dough

1 cup (2 sticks) butter, softened

¾ cup sugar

1 egg yolk, lightly beaten

2 teaspoons vanilla extract

2 cups all-purpose flour

1 teaspoon ground cinnamon

Pinch of salt

½ cup dried blueberries

½ cup dried cranberries

½ cup pine nuts, chopped

Directions

• Preheat the oven to 375°F.

• Line several baking sheets with parchment paper.

• Place the butter and sugar in a large bowl and beat together until light and fluffy, then beat in the egg yolk and vanilla extract.

• Sift together the flour, cinnamon, and salt into the mixture. Add the blueberries and cranberries and stir until thoroughly combined.

• Spread out the chopped pine nuts in a shallow dish.

• Scoop up tablespoons of the mixture and roll them into balls. Roll the balls in the pine nuts to coat, then place on the baking sheets, spaced well apart, and flatten slightly.

• Bake in the preheated oven for 10–15 minutes.

• Let cool on the baking sheets for 5–10 minutes, then transfer the cookies to wire racks to cool completely.

Midnight Cookies

Makes about 25 cookies

Dough

½ cup (1 stick) butter, softened

1 cup sugar

1 egg, lightly beaten

½ teaspoon vanilla extract

1 cup all-purpose flour

⅓ cup unsweetened cocoa

½ teaspoon baking soda

Directions

- Preheat the oven to 350°F.

- Line several baking sheets with parchment paper.

- Place the butter and sugar in a large bowl and beat together until light and fluffy. Add the egg and vanilla extract and mix until smooth. Sift in the flour, cocoa, and baking soda and beat until well mixed.

- With dampened hands, roll walnut-size pieces of the dough into smooth balls. Place on the baking sheets, spaced well apart.

- Bake in the preheated oven for 10–12 minutes, or until set.

- Let cool on the baking sheets for 5 minutes, then transfer the cookies to wire racks to cool completely.

White Chocolate Cookies

Makes about 30 cookies

Dough

½ cup (1 stick) butter

½ cup firmly packed light brown sugar

1 egg, lightly beaten

1¾ cups self-rising flour

Pinch of salt

¾ cup white chocolate pieces

⅓ cup chopped Brazil nuts

Directions

• Preheat the oven to 375°F.

• Grease several baking sheets.

• Place the butter and sugar in a large bowl and beat together until light and fluffy. Gradually add the egg, beating well.

• Sift the flour and salt into the creamed mixture and blend well. Stir in the white chocolate chunks and chopped nuts.

• Place teaspoonfuls of the batter on the baking sheets, putting no more than 6 on each sheet because the cookies will spread during cooking.

• Bake in the preheated oven for 10–12 minutes, or until just golden brown.

• Transfer the cookies to wire racks to cool completely.

Chocolate Chip Cookies

Makes about 30 cookies

Dough

2¼ cups all-purpose flour

1 teaspoon baking soda

1 teaspoon salt

1 cup (2 sticks) butter

¾ cup firmly packed light brown sugar

¾ cup sugar

1 teaspoon vanilla extract

2 large eggs

2 cups semisweet chocolate chips

1 cup chopped walnuts (optional)

Directions

• Preheat oven to 375°F.

• Line several baking sheets with parchment paper.

• Add the flour, baking soda and salt to a small mixing bowl and mix together. Set aside.

• In another bowl, beat the butter, brown sugar, white sugar, and vanilla extract until light and fluffy.

• Add the eggs one at a time, beating thoroughly after each addition. Stir in the flour mixture until combined. Stir in the chocolate chips and nuts (optional). Mix the dough well.

• Drop the cookie dough by rounded tablespoons on prepared baking sheets about 3-inches apart.

• Bake for about 10 minutes, or until lightly browned around the edges.

• Let sit on the baking sheets for 2 minutes, and then remove to wire cooling racks to cool completely.

Banana & Chocolate Cookies

Makes about 20 cookies

Dough

½ cup (1 stick) butter

⅔ cup sugar

1 large egg

1 ripe banana, mashed

1 teaspoon apple pie spice

1¼ cups self-rising flour

2 tablespoons milk

⅓ cup chocolate chips

⅓ cup raisins

Directions

• Preheat oven to 375°F.

• Line several baking sheets with parchment paper.

• Add the flour, and apple pie spice together and set aside.

• Place the butter and sugar in a bowl and beat together until light and fluffy. Gradually add the egg, beating well after each addition.

• Mash the banana and add to the mixture, beating well.

• Fold the flour and spice into the mixture with a spatula. Add the milk and then fold in the chocolate pieces and raisins.

• Drop the cookie dough by rounded tablespoons on prepared baking sheets about 3-inches apart.

• Bake for about 15 minutes, or until lightly browned around the edges.

• Let sit on the baking sheets for 2 minutes, and then remove to wire cooling racks to cool completely.

Checkerboard Cookies

Makes about 20 cookies

Dough

1 cup (2 sticks) butter, softened

¾ cup sugar

1 egg yolk

2 teaspoons vanilla extract

2 cups all-purpose flour

Pinch of salt

1 teaspoon ground ginger

1 tablespoon finely grated orange rind

1 tablespoon unsweetened cocoa

1 egg white

Directions

• Preheat the oven to 375°F.

• Line several baking sheets with parchment paper.

• Place the butter and sugar in a large bowl and beat together until light and fluffy. Add the egg yolk and vanilla extract and mix until smooth. Sift in the flour and salt and stir until combined.

• Divide the dough in half. Add the ginger and orange rind to one half and mix well. Shape the dough into a log 6 inches long. Flatten the sides and top to make a square. Wrap in plastic wrap and chill for 30 minutes.

• Sift the cocoa into the other half of the dough and mix well. Shape into a log as per previous dough. Wrap in plastic wrap and chill for 30 minutes.

• Unwrap both doughs and cut each log lenghwise into 3 slices. Cut each slice lengthwise into 3 strips. Brush the strips with egg white and stack them in threes, alternating the colors until they are the same shape as the original log. Wrap and chill for 30 minutes.

• Unwrap and slice the dough. Bake in the preheated oven for 10–12 minutes, or until set.

• Let cool on the baking sheets for 5 minutes, then transfer the cookies to wire racks to cool completely.

Mixed Fruit Cookies

Makes about 26 cookies

Dough

1 cup (2 sticks) butter, softened

¾ cup sugar

1 egg yolk

2½ cups all-purpose flour

½ teaspoon apple pie spice

¼ cup chopped dried apple

¼ cup chopped dried pear (or apricots)

¼ cup chopped dried prunes

Grated rind of 1 orange

Pinch salt

Directions

• Preheat the oven to 375°F.

• Line several baking sheets with parchment paper.

• Place the butter and sugar in a large bowl and beat together until light and fluffy. Add the egg yolk and and beat until smooth. Sift in the flour, apple pie spice, salt and stir until combined.

• Add all the dried fruits and mix until thoroughly combined. Shape the dough into a log and wrap in plastic wrap and chill for 30 minutes.

• Unwrap the dough and cut into slices. Put them on the prepared baking sheet, spaced well apart.

• Bake in the preheated oven for 10–12 minutes, or until golden on the edges.

• Let cool on the baking sheets for 5 minutes, then transfer the cookies to wire racks to cool completely.

Pies

Lemon Meringue Pie

Serves 8

Filling

3 tablespoons cornstarch

½ cup sugar

Grated rind of 3 lemons

1¼ cups cold water

⅔ cup lemon juice

3 egg yolks

4 tablespoons butter, diced

Meringue

3 egg whites

1 cup sugar

Pie Crust

1 ready-made pie crust

Directions

- Preheat oven to 400°F. Grease a 10-inch fluted tart dish.

- Roll out the pastry on a lightly-floured surface into a circle 2 inches larger than the tart pan. Ease the pastry into the tart pan and press down lightly into the corners and trim the edge. Prick the base with a fork and chill in the refrigerator for 20–30 minutes.

- Line the pastry shell with parchment paper and fill with pie weights. Bake on a preheated baking sheet for 15 minutes. Remove the weights and paper and return to the oven for 10 minutes, or until the pastry is dry and just colored. Remove from the oven and reduce the temperature to 300°F.

- To make the filling, put the cornstarch, sugar, and lemon rind in a pan. Gradually add the remaining water and the lemon juice. Bring the mixture to a boil, stirring constantly. Simmer until smooth and glossy.

- Remove from the heat and beat in the egg yolks, one at a time, then beat in the butter. Leave to cool before spooning into the pastry shell.

- For the meringue, whisk the egg whites with an electric mixer until soft peaks form. Add the sugar gradually, whisking well with each addition. Spoon over the filling. Swirl the meringue into peaks. Bake for 20–30 minutes, or until the meringue is crispy and pale gold but still soft in the center. Cool before serving.

Candied Sweet Potato Pie

Serves 8

Pie Crust

1¼ cups all-purpose flour

½ teaspoon salt

¼ teaspoon sugar

1½ tablespoons butter, diced

3 tablespoons vegetable shortening

2–2½ tablespoons ice-cold water

Filling

2 cups mashed cooked sweet potatoes

3 extra-large eggs, beaten

½ cup firmly packed dark brown sugar

1½ cups evaporated milk

3 tablespoons butter, melted

2 teaspoons vanilla extract

1 teaspoon ground cinnamon

1 teaspoon ground nutmeg

½ teaspoon salt

Freshly whipped cream, to serve

Directions

• Preheat oven to 425°F. Grease a 9-inch pie pan.

• To make the pie crust, sift the flour, salt, and sugar into a bowl. Add the butter and vegetable shortening to the bowl and rub in with the fingertips until fine crumbs form. Sprinkle over 2 tablespoons of the water and mix with a fork until a soft dough forms. Wrap in plastic wrap and chill for at least 1 hour.

• To make the filling, put the sweet potatoes into a separate bowl and beat in the eggs and sugar until very smooth. Beat in the remaining ingredients, except the whipped cream, then set aside.

• Roll out the dough on a lightly floured surface into a thin 11-inch circle and line the pie pan. Trim off the

excess dough and press the floured lines of a fork around the edge.

• Prick the base of the pastry shell all over with the fork and place crumpled kitchen foil in the center. Bake for 12 minutes, or until golden.

• Remove the pastry shell from the oven, take out the foil, pour the filling into the shell, and return to the oven for an additional 10 minutes. Reduce the oven temperature to 325°F and bake for a further 35 minutes, or until a knife inserted into the center comes out clean.

• Let cool on a cooling rack. Serve warm or at room temperature with whipped cream.

Spiced Pumpkin Pie

Serves 8

Pie Crust
1 cup all-purpose flour
¼ teaspoon baking powder
Pinch ground cinnamon
Pinch ground nutmeg
Pinch ground cloves
1 teaspoon salt
½ cup sugar
4 tablespoons unsalted butter
1 egg

Filling
1 can pumpkin puree

1¾ cups condensed milk
2 eggs
1 teaspoon pumpkin pie spice
½ teaspoon vanilla extract
1 tablespoon light brown sugar

Topping
2 tablespoons all-purpose flour
4 tablespoons light brown sugar
1 teaspoon pumpkin pie spice
2 tablespoons unsalted butter
⅔ cup chopped pecans
⅔ cup chopped walnuts

Directions

• Preheat the oven to 425°F. Grease a 9-inch round pie pan.

• To make the pie crust, sift the flour and baking powder into a large bowl. Stir in the cinnamon, nutmeg, cloves, and salt, and all the sugar.

• Rub in the butter with your fingertips until the mixture resembles fine breadcrumbs, then make a well in the center. Lightly beat one of the eggs and pour it into the well. Mix together with a wooden spoon, then use your hands to shape the dough into a ball.

• Place the dough on a lightly floured surface and roll out to a round large enough to line the pie pan. Use it

to line the pan, then trim the edges. Cover with plastic wrap and chill in the refrigerator for 30 minutes.

• To make the filling, put the pumpkin puree in a large bowl. Stir in the condensed milk and the eggs. Add the pumpkin pie spices, then stir in the vanilla extract and brown sugar. Pour into the pastry shell and bake in the preheated oven for 15 minutes.

• To make the topping, combine the flour, brown sugar, and spice in a bowl. Rub in the butter, then stir in the nuts.

• Remove the pie from the oven and reduce the heat to 350°F. Sprinkle the topping over the pie and bake for an additional 35 minutes.

Simple Apple Pie

Serves 8

Pie Crust

2 ready-made pie crusts, thaw if frozen

1 beaten egg to glaze the pastry

Filling

6 baking apples (6 cups) peeled and sliced

⅓ cup lemon juice

1 cup sugar

3 tablespoons cornstarch

Pinch of nutmeg

½ teaspoon cinnamon

2 tablespoons butter

Directions

• Preheat oven to 375°F.

• Grease a 9-inch pie pan.

• Roll one dough on a lightly floured surface to form the bottom crust. It should be rolled large enough to cover the pan with a few inches to spare all around. Place and press into the pan.

• For the filling, peel, core, and slice the apples into thin slices. Toss the apple slices with the lemon juice in a large mixing bowl. Add the rest of the filling ingredients, except the butter, and mix until well combined.

• Pour the apple mixture into the bottom crust. Dot the top of the apples with the butter.

• Roll out the second pie crust and cover the mounded apples.

• Press the two pieces of dough together with your fingers. Pinch the edges so that both crusts are sealed all the way around the pan.

• Cut a few slashes in the top crust so the steam can escape. Brush the top crust with the beaten egg. Bake for 1-1½ hours, until the crust is nicely browned, and the apples are tender when tested with a small knife through the slits on the top. If the crust begins to brown too quickly, tent with foil.

• Serve warm or cooled.

Cherry Pie

Serves 8

Pie Crust

1 cup all-purpose flour

¼ teaspoon baking powder

½ teaspoon allspice

½ teaspoon salt

¼ cup sugar

4 tablespoons unsalted butter

1 egg, beaten, plus extra for glazing

Filling

4 cups (2 lbs) pitted fresh cherries
or drained canned cherries

½ cup sugar

½ teaspoon almond extract

2 teaspoons cherry brandy

¼ teaspoon allspice

2 tablespoons cornstarch

2 tablespoons water

2 tablespoons unsalted butter

Directions

• Preheat the oven to 425°F. Grease a 9-inch round tart pan.

• To make the pie crusts, sift the flour and baking powder into a large bowl. Stir in the allspice, salt, and sugar. Rub in the butter with your fingertips until the mixture resembles fine breadcrumbs. Add the beaten egg and mix to a firm dough. Cut the dough in half and roll each half into a ball. Roll out one half of the dough and line the pan.

• To make the filling, put half of the cherries and the sugar in a large saucepan. Bring to a simmer over low heat, stirring, until the sugar has dissolved. Stir in the almond extract, brandy, and allspice. In a separate bowl, mix the cornstarch and water to form a paste. Remove the

saucepan from the heat, stir in the cornstarch paste, then return to the heat and stir continuously until the mixture boils. Stir in the remaining cherries, pour into the pastry shell.

• Cut the remaining dough into long strips about ½ inch wide. Lay five strips evenly across the top of the filling. Now lay six strips crosswise over the strips, folding back every other strip each time you add another crosswise strip, to form a lattice. Trim off the ends and seal the edges with water. Use your fingers to crimp around the rim, then brush the top with beaten egg to glaze.

• Cover with foil and bake for 30 minutes. Discard the foil, then bake for an additional 15 minutes, or until the crust is golden.

Pecan Pie

Serves 8

Pie Crust

1¾ cups all-purpose flour

½ cup (1 stick) butter

2 tablespoons sugar

Filling

6 tablespoons butter

½ cup firmly packed dark brown sugar

⅔ cup dark corn syrup

2 extra-large eggs, beaten

1 teaspoon vanilla extract

1 cup pecans

Directions

• Preheat oven to 400°F.

• Grease a 9-inch spring form tart pan.

• For the pie crust, place the flour in a bowl and rub in the butter using your fingertips until it resembles fine breadcrumbs. Stir in the sugar and add enough cold water to mix to a firm dough. Wrap in plastic wrap and chill for 15 minutes, until firm enough to roll out.

• Roll out the dough on a lightly-floured surface and use to line the 9-inch tart pan. Prick the bottom with a fork. Chill for 15 minutes.

• Place the tart pan on a baking sheet, line the crust with a sheet of parchment paper, and fill with pie weights. Bake in the preheated oven for 10 minutes. Remove the paper and weights and bake for an additional 5 minutes. Reduce the oven temperature to 350°F.

• For the filling, place the butter, brown sugar, and corn syrup in a saucepan and heat gently until melted. Remove from the heat and quickly beat in the eggs and vanilla extract.

• Coarsely chop the pecans and stir into the mixture. Pour into the tart shell and bake for 35–40 minutes, until the filling is just set. Serve warm or cold.

Mississippi Mud Pie

Serves 8

Pie Crust

1½ cups all-purpose flour

2 tablespoons unsweetened cocoa

½ cup (1 stick) unsalted butter

2 tablespoons sugar

1–2 tablespoons cold water

Filling

¾ cup (1¾ stick) unsalted butter

1¾ cups firmly packed dark brown sugar

4 eggs, lightly beaten

4 tablespoons unsweetened cocoa, sifted

1 cup semisweet chocolate pieces

1¼ cups light cream

Decoration

2 cups heavy cream, whipped

chocolate flakes and curls

Directions

- Preheat the oven to 375°F. Grease a 9-inch round tart pan.

- To make the crust, sift the flour and cocoa into a mixing bowl. Rub in the butter with your fingertips until the mixture resembles fine breadcrumbs. Stir in the sugar and enough cold water to mix to a soft dough. Wrap the dough in plastic wrap and let chill in the refrigerator for 15 minutes.

- Roll out the dough on a lightly floured surface and use to line the pan. Line with parchment paper and fill with pie weights. Bake for 15 minutes. Remove from the oven and take out the paper and weights. Bake the pastry shell for an additional 10 minutes.

- To make the filling, beat the butter and sugar together in a bowl and gradually beat in the eggs with the cocoa. Melt the chocolate in a heatproof bowl set over a saucepan of gently simmering water, then beat it into the mixture with the light cream.

- Reduce the oven temperature to 325°F. Pour the filling into the pastry shell and bake for 45 minutes, or until the filling has set gently.

- Let the pie cool completely, then transfer it to a serving plate. Cover with the whipped cream. Decorate with chocolate flakes and curls and chill until ready to serve.

Key Lime Pie

Serves 8

Pie crust

2 cups graham crackers, crushed

2 tablespoons sugar

½ teaspoon ground cinnamon

6 tablespoons butter

Filling and Decoration

1¾ cups sweetened condensed milk

½ cup freshly squeezed lime juice

Finely grated rind of 3 limes

4 egg yolks

Whipped cream, to serve

Directions

- Preheat the oven to 325°F.

- Lightly grease a 9-inch round tart pan.

- To make the crumb crust, place the crackers, sugar, and cinnamon in a food processor and process until fine crumbs form. Do not overprocess to a powder. Add the melted butter and process again until moistened.

- Tip the crumb mixture into the prepared tart pan and press over the bottom and sides. Place the tart pan on a baking sheet and bake in the preheated oven for 5 minutes.

- Meanwhile, beat the condensed milk, lime juice, lime rind, and egg yolks together in a bowl until well blended.

- Remove the tart pan from the oven, pour in the filling, and spread out to the edges. Return to the oven for an additional 15 minutes, or until the filling is set around the edges but still wobbly in the center.

- Let cool completely on a wire rack, then cover and let chill for at least 2 hours. Serve spread thickly with freshly whipped cream.

Really Rich Chocolate Tartlets

Serves 8

Pie Crust

1⅔ cups all-purpose flour

½ cup (1 stick) butter cut into cubes

2 tablespoons confectioners' sugar

1 egg yolk

2–3 tablespoons cold water

Filling and Decoration

1½ cups semisweet chocolate, pieces

½ cup (1 stick) butter

½ cup confectioners' sugar

1¼ cups heavy cream

Grated chocolate for decorating.

Directions

• Preheat the oven to 400°F.

• Grease eight 4-inch tartlet pans or line with parchment paper.

• Place the flour in a large bowl. Add the butter and rub it in with your fingertips until the mixture resembles breadcrumbs. Add the confectioners' sugar, egg yolk, and enough water to form a soft dough. Cover and chill in the refrigerator for 15 minutes.

• Roll the dough out on a lightly floured work surface. Create eight 6-inch circles and line the tartlet pans. Chill for 30 minutes.

• Prick the bottom of the shells with a fork and line with

a little crumpled foil. Bake in the preheated oven for 10 minutes, then remove the foil and bake for 5–10 minutes, until crisp. Transfer to a wire rack to cool. Reduce the oven temperature to 325°F.

• To make the filling, place the chocolate pieces, butter, and confectioners' sugar in a heat-proof bowl set over a saucepan of simmering water and heat until melted. Remove from the heat and stir in ¾ cup heavy cream. Remove the shells from the pans and place on a baking sheet. Fill each shell with the chocolate. Bake for 5 minutes. Cool, then chill until required.

• To serve, whip the remaining cream and pipe or spoon into the center of each tart. Decorate with grated chocolate.

Fresh Blueberry Pie

Serves 8

Pie Crust

2 cups all-purpose flour

1 cup vegetable shortening

½ teaspoon salt

¼ cup whole milk

2 tablespoons vinegar

Filling

¾ cup sugar

3 tablespoons cornstarch

¼ teaspoon salt

½ teaspoon ground cinnamon

½ teaspoon ground nutmeg

4 cups fresh blueberries

1 tablespoon butter

Directions

• Preheat oven to 425°F.

• Lightly grease a 9-inch pie pan or line with parchment paper.

• Sift the flour and salt into a bowl and cut in the shortening with a pastry blender or your fingertips until it is the size of small peas. Using a fork lightly mix the ingredients. Add the vinegar and milk, just enough to moisten the dry ingredients, being sure to add the milk 1 tablespoon at a time. The dough will be sticky.

• Divide the dough in half and roll out one half on a lightly floured surface to a circle about 12-inches in diameter. Line the pie pan.

• Bake the pastry on lower shelf of oven for about 50 minutes, or until crust is golden brown.

• To make the filling, mix the sugar, cornstarch, salt, cinnamon, nutmeg and sprinkle over the blueberries. Pour the berry mixture into the baked crust, and dot with butter.

• Cut the remaining pastry into ½–¾ inch wide strips, and make a lattice top. Crimp and flute the edges.

• Bake the pie on the lower shelf of the oven for about 50 minutes, or until the crust is golden brown. Serve warm or cooled.

Peach & Almond Pie

Serves 8

Pie Crust

⅔ cup semisweet chocolate pieces

1 ⅔ cups all-purpose flour

½ cup (1 stick) unsalted butter

4 tablespoons ground almonds

Few drops almond extract

1–2 tablespoons cold water

Glaze

4 tablespoons peach (or apricot) preserve

1 tablespoon peach (or apricot) brandy

Filling

1 ½ cup blanched almonds

½ cup sugar

1 tablespoon unsalted butter

2 egg yolks

4 egg whites

1 teaspoon almond extract

5–6 ripe peaches (or apricots)

Directions

- Preheat the oven to 375°F.

- Grease a 9-inch spring-form tart pan.

- To make the pie crust, melt the chocolate in a heatproof bowl set over a pan of barely simmering water. Remove from the heat and let cool slightly. Sift the flour into a bowl and rub in the butter with the fingertips until the mixture resembles bread crumbs. Make a well in the center and add the melted chocolate, ground almonds, almond extract, and enough water to mix to a dough. Knead lightly. Wrap the dough in plastic wrap and let chill in the refrigerator for 30 minutes.

- Roll out the dough on a lightly floured surface and line the pan.

- For the filling, process the blanched almonds and sugar in a food processor, until finely ground. Add the butter and process until smooth. Add the egg yolk, egg whites, and almond extract and process until combined.

- Peel, halve, and pit the peaches. Thinly slice the peach halves crosswise. Spoon the almond mixture into the tart shell and transfer the sliced peach halves onto the top of the almond mixture.

- Bake for 50 minutes, or until set and golden brown.

- To make the glaze, heat the preserve and brandy in a small pan, stirring until melted. Brush the glaze over the top of the pie and serve warm.

Three Berry Pie

Serves 8

Pie Crust

1½ cups all-purpose flour

¼ cup ground hazelnuts

½ cup (1 stick) butter, softened

⅓ cup sugar

Finely grated rind of 1 lemon

1 egg yolk, beaten

3 tablespoons whole milk

Filling

1½ cups blueberries

1½ cups raspberries

1½ cups blackberries

3 tablespoons sugar

2 tablespoons whole milk

Directions

• Preheat the oven to 375°F. Grease a 9-inch pie pan with butter.

• To make the pie crust, sift the flour into a bowl, then add the hazelnuts. Rub in the butter with fingertips until the mixture resembles bread crumbs, then sift in the sugar. Add the lemon rind, egg yolk, and milk and mix.

• Turn out onto a lightly floured counter and knead briefly. Wrap in plastic wrap and let chill in the refrigerator for 30 minutes.

• Roll out two-thirds of the pie dough to a thickness of ¼ inch and use it to line the base and side of the pan.

• To make the filling, place the fruit in a pan with the sugar and let simmer stirring frequently, for 5 minutes. Remove the pan from the heat.

• Spoon the fruit into the pastry shell. Roll out the remaining pie dough to cover the pie. Trim and crimp round the edge, then make 2 small slits in the top and decorate with 2 leaf shapes cut out from the dough trimmings. Brush with a little milk and bake for 40 minutes or until the crust is golden brown.

• Serve warm or cooled.

Chocolate Pumpkin Pie

Serves 8

Pie Crust

2 cups finely ground graham crackers

6 tablespoons butter, melted

1 tablespoon sugar

2 tablespoons firmly packed light brown sugar

½ teaspoon salt

½ teaspoon ground cinnamon

¼ cup bittersweet chocolate, chopped

Filling

¾ cup semisweet chocolate, pieces

4 tablespoons unsalted butter

1 can pumpkin puree

1 can evaporated milk

¾ cup firmly packed light brown sugar

3 large eggs

1 tablespoon cornstarch

2 teaspoons vanilla extract

1½ teaspoons salt

2 teaspoons pumpkin pie spice

Directions

• Preheat oven to 350°F and grease a 9-inch pie pan.

• To make the crust, combine the graham cracker crumbs, butter, sugars, salt, and cinnamon in a bowl. Firmly press the mixture into the bottom and up thesides of the pie pan Bake until firm, 8 to 10 minutes.

• Remove from the oven, and sprinkle the bittersweet chocolate over bottom of crust. Return to the oven to melt the chocolate, about 1 minute. Spread the chocolate in a thin layer on the bottom and up the sides. Let cool on a wire rack and reduce the oven temperature to 325°F degrees.

• To make the filling, in a large heatproof bowl set over a pot of simmering water, melt the semisweet chocolate

and butter, stirring until smooth. Remove from the heat.

• Mix the pumpkin puree, milk, brown sugar, eggs, cornstarch, vanilla, salt, and pumpkin pie spice in a medium bowl. Whisk ⅓ pumpkin mixture into chocolate mixture. Whisk in remaining pumpkin mixture until completely incorporated.

• Transfer the pie pan to a rimmed baking sheet, and pour the pumpkin mixture into crust. Bake until the center is set but still a bit wobbly, 55–60 minutes. Let cool in pie dish on a wire rack.

• Refrigerate until well chilled, at least 8 hours (preferably overnight). Serve cold.

Lemon Sponge Pie

Serves 8

Pie Crust

1 ready made pie crust

Filling

2 eggs

6 tablespoons butter

1 cup sugar

2 teaspoons finely grated lemon peel

¼ cup lemon juice

2 tablespoons all-purpose flour

Pinch salt

1 cup whole milk

Directions

• Preheat oven to 450°F. Grease a 9-inch pie pan.

• Prepare the crust and line the pie pan. Bake for 8 minutes or until lightly browned. Cool on rack. Reduce oven temperature to 425°F.

• To make the filling, separate the egg yolks from the whites. Place the whites in a medium bowl and set aside.

• In a large bowl beat the butter with an electric mixer until fluffy. Add the sugar and beat until combined. Beat in the egg yolks, lemon peel, lemon juice, flour, and salt until just combined. Add milk; beat until just combined (the mixture will be thin and will appear curdled).

• In a medium bowl beat the egg whites with an electric mixer until stiff peaks form. Fold the egg whites into the beaten mixture. Transfer the mixture to the prebaked crust.

• Loosely tent the top of the pie with foil to prevent overbrowning, making sure the foil does not touch the filling.

• Bake for 10 minutes before reducing the heat to 350°F and baking for a further 20–25 minutes. The pie will be ready when the center is solid and the slightly golden.

• Serve warm.

Indulgent Cakes & Desserts

Mocha Layer Cake

Serves 8-10

Batter

1¾ cups self-rising flour

¼ teaspoon baking powder

4 tablespoons unsweetened cocoa

½ cup sugar

2 eggs

2 tablespoons corn syrup

⅔ cup vegetable oil

⅔ cup whole milk

Frosting

1 teaspoon instant coffee powder

1 tablespoon boiling water

1¼ cups heavy cream

2 tablespoons confectioners' sugar

Decoration

¼ cup grated chocolate

Confectioners' sugar, for dusting

Directions

• Preheat the oven to 350°F.

• Grease three 8-inch layer cake pans and line with parchment paper.

• To make the cake batter, sift the flour, baking powder, and unsweetened cocoa into a large mixing bowl. Stir in the sugar. Make a well in the center and stir in the eggs, corn syrup, oil, and milk. Beat with a wooden spoon, gradually mixing in the dry ingredients to make a smooth batter.

• Divide the cake batter among the prepared pans. Bake in the preheated oven for 35–45 minutes, or until springy to the touch. Let cool in the pans for 5 minutes, then turn out onto a wire rack to finish cooling.

• For the filling and topping, dissolve the instant coffee in the boiling water and place in a bowl with the cream and confectioners' sugar. Whip until the cream is just holding its shape.

• Use half of the cream to sandwich the 3 cakes together. Spread the remaining cream over the top and sides of the cake.

• To decorate, lightly press the grated chocolate into the cream around the edge of the cake. Transfer to a serving plate. Lay the grated chocolate over the top of the cake and dust lightly with confectioners' sugar.

Chocolate Chiffon Tart

Serves 8-10

Filling

1 cup whole milk

2 teaspoons powdered gelatin

½ cup sugar

2 eggs, separated

1¼ cup semisweet chocolate pieces

1 teaspoon vanilla extract

⅔ cup heavy cream

Nut base

2 cups shelled Brazil nuts

4 tablespoons sugar

4 tablespoons melted butter

Decoration

2 tablespoons chopped Brazil nuts

Directions

- Preheat the oven to 400°F and grease a 9-inch tart pan.

- To make the nut base, place the shelled Brazil nuts in a food processor and process until ground. Add the sugar and melted butter and process to combine.

- Tip the mixture into the pan and press it onto the base and side with a spoon. Bake in the preheated oven for 8–10 minutes, or until light golden brown. Set aside to cool.

- For the filling, pour the milk into a heatproof bowl and sprinkle the gelatin over the surface. Let it soften for 2 minutes, then set over a pan of gently simmering water. Stir in half of the sugar, both the egg yolks, and the chocolate. Stir constantly over a low heat for

4–5 minutes until the gelatin has dissolved and the chocolate has melted. Remove from the heat and beat until the mixture is smooth. Stir in the vanilla extract and chill in the refrigerator for 45–60 minutes.

- Whip the cream until it stiff and peaks form. Fold all but 3 tablespoons into the chocolate mixture.

- Whisk the egg whites in a separate bowl until soft peaks form. Add 2 teaspoons of the remaining sugar and whisk until stiff peaks form. Fold in the remaining sugar, then fold the egg whites into the chocolate mixture. Pour the filling into the pastry shell and chill in the refrigerator for 3 hours. Decorate the pie with the remaining whipped cream and the chopped nuts before serving.

Chocolate Fudge Cake

Serves 8-10

Batter

¾ cup (1½ sticks) butter, softened

1 cup sugar

3 eggs, beaten

3 tablespoons dark corn syrup

3 tablespoons ground almonds

1 cup self-rising flour

Pinch of salt

¼ cup unsweetened cocoa

Frosting

1¼ cups semisweet chocolate pieces

¼ cup firmly packed light brown sugar

1 cup (2 sticks) butter, diced

5 tablespoons evaporated milk

½ teaspoon vanilla extract

Directions

• Preheat the oven to 350°F.

• Grease and line two 8-inch round cake pans with parchment paper.

• To make the batter, place the butter and sugar in a bowl and beat together until light and fluffy. Gradually beat in the eggs. Stir in the corn syrup and ground almonds. Sift the flour, salt, and cocoa into a separate bowl, then fold into the cake batter. Add a little water, if necessary, to make a dropping consistency.

• Spoon the cake batter into the prepared pans and bake in the preheated oven for 30–35 minutes, or until springy to the touch and a toothpick inserted in the center comes out clean.

• Let stand in the pans for 5 minutes, then turn out onto wire racks to cool completely.

• To make the frosting, place the chocolate, brown sugar, butter, evaporated milk, and vanilla extract in a heavy-bottom pan. Heat gently, stirring continuously, until melted. Pour into a bowl and let cool. Cover and let chill in the refrigerator for 1 hour.

• When the cakes have cooled, sandwich them together with half the frosting. Spread the remaining frosting over the top and sides of the cake, swirling it to give a wavy appearance.

Coffee & Walnut Swirl

Serves 6-8

Batter

3 eggs

1 egg white

½ cup sugar

1 teaspoon coffee extract

½ cup all-purpose flour, sifted

¼ cup finely chopped walnuts

Filling

¾ cup heavy cream

⅓ cup confectioners' sugar

1 tablespoon coffee liqueur

Directions

• Preheat the oven to 400°F.

• Grease a 13x9-inch jelly roll pan and line with parchment paper.

• To make the batter, place the eggs, egg white, and sugar in a bowl over a pan of very hot water. Whisk with an electric mixer until pale and thick enough to leave a trail.

• Whisk in the coffee extract, then fold in the flour and the finely chopped walnuts lightly with a metal spoon.

• Spoon the batter into the prepared pan, spreading evenly. Bake in the preheated oven for 12–15 minutes, until golden brown and firm.

• Sprinkle a sheet of parchment paper with sugar. Turn out the sponge onto the paper and peel off the parchment paper. Trim the edges.

• Quickly roll up the sponge from one short side, with the paper inside. Cool completely.

• For the filling, place the cream, sugar, and liqueur in a bowl and whisk until the mixture begins to hold its shape.

• Carefully unroll the sponge, remove the paper and spread the cream filling over. Roll up carefully.

• Serve dusted with confectioners' sugar and topped with roughly chopped walnuts.

Banana Crunch Cake

Serves 8-10

Batter

1 small can crushed pineapple (in juice)

2¼ cups all-purpose flour

1¼ cups sugar

1 teaspoon ground cinnamon

1 teaspoon baking soda

3 eggs, beaten

1 cup vegetable oil

1 cup pecans, coarsely chopped

1 cup mashed ripe bananas

Frosting

¾ cup cream cheese

½ cup (1 stick) unsalted butter

1 teaspoon vanilla extract

3½ cups confectioners' sugar

Directions

- Preheat the oven to 350°F.

- Lightly grease three 9-inch round layer cake pans and line with parchment paper.

- Drain the pineapple, reserving 4 tablespoons of the juice. Set aside.

- To make the batter, sift together the flour, sugar, cinnamon, and baking soda into a large bowl. Add the eggs, oil, pecans, bananas, pineapple, and pineapple juice, and stir with a wooden spoon until evenly mixed.

- Divide the mixture among the prepared pans, spreading evenly. Bake in the preheated oven for

25–30 minutes, or until golden brown and firm to the touch.

- Remove the cakes from the oven and let cool for 10 minutes in the pans before turning out onto wire racks to cool.

- For the frosting, beat together the cream cheese, butter, and vanilla extract in a bowl until smooth. Sift in the confectioners' sugar and mix until smooth.

- Sandwich the cakes together with half of the frosting, spread the remaining frosting over the top, then sprinkle with chopped pecans to decorate.

Carrot Cake

Serves 8-10

Batter

1½ cups all-purpose flour

1 tablespoon baking powder

1 teaspoon ground cinnamon

½ teaspoon ground ginger

¾ cup (1½ sticks) unsalted butter

¾ cup firmly packed light brown sugar

3 eggs, beaten

2 tablespoon orange juice

1½ cups coarsely grated carrots

½ cup chopped pecans

Frosting

¼ cup cream cheese

2¼ cups confectioners' sugar

Finely grated rind of 1 orange

1 tablespoon orange juice

Pecan halves, to decorate

Directions

• Preheat the oven to 325°F.

• Grease and line a 9-inch round cake pan with parchment paper.

• To make the batter, sift the flour, baking powder, cinnamon, and ginger into a bowl and add the butter, sugar, and eggs. Beat well until smooth, then stir in the orange juice, carrots, and chopped pecans.

• Spoon the mixture into the prepared pan and spread the top level. Bake in the preheated oven for 1 hour–1 hour 10 minutes, or until well risen, firm, and golden brown.

• Let cool in the pan for 10 minutes, then turn out onto a wire rack to finish cooling.

• For the frosting, put all the ingredients, except the pecan halves, into a bowl and beat until smooth and thick, adding more orange juice if necessary. Spread over the top of the cake and decorate with pecan halves.

Rich Chocolate Layer Cake

Serves 8-10

Batter

½ cup semisweet chocolate pieces

2 tablespoons whole milk

1½ cups all-purpose flour

1 tablespoon baking powder

¾ cup (1½ sticks) unsalted butter

¾ cup firmly packed light brown sugar

3 eggs, beaten

1 teaspoon vanilla extract

Frosting

1½ cups semisweet chocolate pieces

1 cup heavy cream

2 tablespoons dark rum

Grated chocolate, to decorate

Directions

• Preheat the oven to 350°F.

• Grease and line three 8-inch round cake pans with parchment paper.

• To make the filling, put the chocolate and milk into a small pan and heat gently, without boiling, until melted. Stir and remove from the heat.

• Sift the flour and baking powder into a large bowl and add the butter, sugar, eggs, and vanilla extract. Beat until smooth, then stir in the chocolate mixture.

• Divide the mixture among the prepared pans and smooth the tops level. Bake for 20–25 minutes, or until risen and firm to the touch.

• Let cool in the pans for 5 minutes, then turn out and finish cooling on wire racks.

• For the frosting, melt the chocolate with the cream and rum in a small pan over low heat. Remove from the heat and let cool, stirring occasionally, until it reaches a spreadable consistency.

• Sandwich the cakes together with about a third of the frosting, then spread the remainder over the top and sides of the cake, swirling with a spatula. Sprinkle with grated chocolate and let set.

Strawberry Layer Cake

Serves 6-8

Batter

1⅓ cups all-purpose flour

1½ teaspoons baking powder

¾ cup (1½ sticks) unsalted butter

¾ cup sugar

3 eggs, beaten

1 teaspoon vanilla extract

2 tablespoons whole milk

Filling

2 cups fresh strawberries

1 cup mascarpone cheese

Confectioners' sugar, for dusting

Directions

• Preheat the oven to 350°F.

• Grease a 9x13-inch jelly roll pan and line with parchment paper.

• To make the batter, sift the flour and baking powder into a large bowl and add the butter, sugar, eggs, and vanilla extract. Beat well until the mixture is smooth, then beat in the milk.

• Spoon the mixture into the prepared pan and smooth into the corners with a spatula. Bake in the preheated oven for 15–20 minutes, or until risen, firm, and golden brown. Let cool in the pan.

• When the cake is cold, cut crosswise into three rectangles. Hull and chop the strawberries, reserving 4 for decoration. Stir the chopped strawberries into the mascarpone and use to sandwich together the cakes.

• To serve, dust the cake with confectioners' sugar. Hull and slice the reserved strawberries and arrange on top.

Double Chocolate Mint Cake

Serves 8-10

Batter

1¼ cups all-purpose flour

2 tablespoons unsweetened cocoa

1 tablespoon baking powder

¾ cup (¾ stick) unsalted butter

1 cup sugar

3 eggs, beaten

1 tablespoon whole milk

12 chocolate mint sticks, chopped

Filling and Decoration

⅔ cup chocolate spread

Chocolate mint sticks to decorate

Directions

- Preheat the oven to 350°F.

- Grease two 8-inch layer cake pans and line with parchment paper.

- To make the batter, sift the flour, unsweetened cocoa, and baking powder into a bowl and beat in the butter, sugar, and eggs, mixing until smooth. Stir in the milk and chocolate mint pieces.

- Spread the batter into the pans. Bake for 25–30 minutes, until risen and firm. Cool in the pan for 2 minutes, then turn out onto a wire rack to finish cooling.

- Sandwich the cakes together with the chocolate spread, then drizzle more chocolate spread over the top.

- Decorate the cake with chocolate mint sticks.

White Chocolate Mocha Cake

Serves 8-10

Batter

3 tablespoons unsalted butter

½ cup white chocolate pieces

⅔ cup sugar

4 extra-large eggs, beaten

2 tablespoons very strong black coffee

1 teaspoon vanilla extract

1 cup all-purpose flour

Frosting

1 cup white chocolate pieces

6 tablespoons unsalted butter

½ cup sour cream

1 cup confectioners' sugar, sifted

1 tablespoon coffee liqueur or very strong black coffee

White chocolate curls, to decorate

Directions

• Preheat the oven to 350°F. Grease two 8-inch cake pans and line with parchment paper.

• Before making the batter place the butter and chocolate in a bowl set over a saucepan of hot, but not simmering, water and leave on very low heat until just melted.

• To make the batter, place the sugar, eggs, coffee, and vanilla extract in a large bowl set over a saucepan of hot water and beat with an electric mixer until the mixture is pale and thick.

• Remove from the heat, sift in the flour. Fold in the butter and chocolate mixture, and divide between the prepared pans.

• Bake for 25–30 minutes, until risen, golden brown, and springy to the touch. Cool in the pans for 2 minutes before turning out onto a wire rack to cool.

• For the frosting, place the chocolate and butter in a bowl set over a saucepan of hot water and heat gently until melted. Remove from the heat, stir in the sour cream, then add the confectioners' sugar and coffee liqueur and mix until smooth. Chill the frosting for at least 30 minutes, stirring occasionally, until it becomes thick and glossy.

• Use about one third of the frosting to sandwich the cakes together. Spread the remainder over the top and sides, swirling with a spatula. Arrange the chocolate curls over the top of the cake and let set.

Pumpkin Sandwich Cake

Serves 8-10

Batter

¾ cup all-purpose flour

1½ teaspoons pumpkin pie spice

1 teaspoon baking powder

¼ teaspoon salt

1 cup sugar

¼ cup canned pumpkin

3 eggs

Filling

½ cup whipping cream

½ cup cream cheese

½ cup confectioners' sugar

Frosting

½ cup whipping cream

1 cup bittersweet chocolate pieces

Directions

• Preheat oven to 375°F. Grease two 8-inch round cake pans and line with parchment paper.

• To make the batter, in a large bowl combine the flour, pumpkin pie spice, baking powder and salt; set aside.

• In second bowl, beat eggs and sugar with an electric mixer on medium to high speed until thick, about 5 minutes. Beat in pumpkin. Add to the flour mixture and beat just until combined. Spread the cake batter in the prepared pans.

• Bake for 16–18 minutes or until a toothpick inserted into the center comes out clean. Cool pans on wire rack 10 minutes; remove and cool thoroughly.

• For filling, in a chilled mixing bowl beat the whipping cream to soft peaks; set aside. In a second mixing bowl beat the cream cheese until smooth and mix in the sugar. Finally fold in the whipped cream.

• To assemble, place one cake layer on a serving platter. Spread the cream cheese mixture evenly over bottom cake layer. Top with the second cake layer.

• For the frosting, In small saucepan bring the whipping cream just to boiling over a medium heat. Remove from the heat and pour over the chocolate pieces Let stand 5 minutes. Stir until smooth. Cool for 15 minutes.

• Spread over top and sides of cake. Sprinkle lightly with pumpkin pie spice or confectioners sugar.

Angel Food Cake

Serves 8-10

Batter

8 extra-large egg whites

1 teaspoon cream of tartar

1 teaspoon almond extract

1¼ cups sugar

1 cup all-purpose flour

Topping

2¼ cups berries, such as strawberries

and raspberries

1 tablespoon lemon juice

2 tablespoons confectioners' sugar

Directions

• Preheat the oven to 325°F.

• Brush the inside of a 9-cup Bundt pan with oil and dust lightly with flour.

• To make the batter, in a large grease-free bowl, whisk the egg whites until they hold soft peaks. Add the cream of tartar and whisk again until the whites are stiff but not dry.

• Whisk in the almond extract, then add the sugar a tablespoon at a time, whisking hard between each addition. Sift in the flour and fold in lightly and evenly.

• Spoon the batter into the prepared cake pan and tap on the counter to remove any large air bubbles. Bake in the preheated oven for 40–45 minutes, or until golden brown and firm to the touch.

• Run the tip of a small knife around the edge of the cake to loosen from the pan. Let cool in the pan for 10 minutes, then turn out onto a wire rack to finish cooling.

• Place the berries, lemon juice, and confectioners' sugar in a saucepan and heat gently until the sugar has dissolved. Serve with the cake.

New York Cheesecake

Serves 8-10

Base

½ cup (1 stick) butter

1¾ cups finely crushed graham crackers

1 tablespoon sugar

Filling

4 cups (2lbs) cream cheese

1¼ cups sugar

2 tablespoons all-purpose flour

1 teaspoon vanilla extract

Finely grated zest of 1 orange

Finely grated zest of 1 lemon

3 eggs

2 egg yolks

1¼ cups heavy cream

Directions

• Preheat the oven to 350°F.

• Grease a 9-inch round cake pan and line with parchment paper.

• To make the pie crust, place a small saucepan over low heat, melt the butter and remove from heat. Stir in crushed crackers and the sugar. Press the cracker mixture into bottom of the cake pan.

• Place in oven and bake for 10 minutes. Remove and cool.

• Increase the oven temperature to 400°F. With an electric mixer beat cream cheese until creamy and gradually add the sugar and flour and beat until smooth.

• Beat in the vanilla extract, orange and lemon zest, then one at a time beat in the eggs and egg yolks. Finally beat in the cream. The mixture should be light and airy.

• Grease the sides of the cake pan and pour in the filling. Transfer to the preheated oven and bake for 15 minutes. Reduce the heat to 200°F and bake for an additional 30 minutes. Turn the oven off and leave to cool for 2 hours.

• Cover with plastic wrap and refrigerate overnight.

Brownie Cheesecake

Serves 8-10

Base

½ cup (1 stick) unsalted butter

⅔ cup semisweet chocolate pieces

1 cup sugar

2 eggs, beaten

¼ cup whole milk

1 cup all-purpose flour

Topping

2¼ cups (1lb) cream cheese

⅔ cup sugar

3 eggs, beaten

1 teaspoon vanilla extract

½ cup plain yogurt

Decoration

Melted chocolate, for drizzling

Chocolate-dipped strawberries, to serve

Directions

• Preheat the oven to 350°F.

• Lightly grease and flour a 9-inch round springform cake pan.

• To make the base, melt the butter and chocolate in a saucepan over low heat, stirring frequently, until smooth. Remove from the heat and beat in the sugar.

• Add the eggs and milk, beating well. Stir in the flour, mixing just until blended. Spoon into the prepared pan, spreading evenly.

• Bake in the preheated oven for 25 minutes. Remove from the oven and reduce the oven temperature to 325°F.

• For the topping, beat together the cream cheese, sugar, eggs, and vanilla extract until well blended. Stir in the yogurt, then pour into the pan. Bake for an additional 45–55 minutes, or until the center is almost set.

• Run a knife around the edge of the cheesecake to loosen from the pan. Let cool before removing from the pan. Chill in the refrigerator for 4 hours or overnight before cutting into slices.

• Drizzle with melted chocolate and serve with chocolate-dipped strawberries.

Party Cakes

Candy Store Cake

Serves 8-10

Carrot Cake

2 cups all-purpose flour

1 cup walnut pieces

2 cups sugar

2 teaspoons baking powder

1 teaspoons baking soda

1 tablespoon ground cinnamon

1 teaspoon salt

3 large eggs

1 cup vegetable oil

2½ cups grated carrots

1 cup canned crushed pineapple, drained

Cream Cheese Coconut Frosting

4 cups (1lb) cream cheese

½ cup (1 stick) unsalted butter

1½ teaspoons vanilla extract

2½ cups confectioners' sugar

2 tablespoons whole milk

½ cup shredded coconut

Decoration

Red food coloring

Assorted candy pieces

Directions

- Preheat the oven to 350°F. Lightly grease two 8-inch round cake pans and line with parchment paper.

- Process the walnuts in a food processor until chopped into pieces and set aside. Combine the sugar, baking soda, baking powder, cinnamon and salt. Slowly add the eggs and oil and beat thoroughly. Finally add the walnut pieces, grated carrot and pineapple. Mix well.

- Pour the mixture into the prepared pans and bake for 60-70 minutes or until a toothpick inserted into the center comes out clean. Allow the cakes to cool.

- To make the frosting, beat the cream cheese, butter and vanilla extract until smooth. Add in the sugar slowly and then stir in the milk and coconut.

- Add two drops of red food coloring until the frosting turns a pale pink color.

- Sandwich the two cakes together with the frosting. Frost the top and sides of the cake. Swirl the frosting to create a wavy look. Refrigerate the cake until needed.

- Remove the cake from the refrigerator and scatter candies over the entire cake. Do not place the cake back in the refrigerator once the candies are in place as the colors will bleed into the frosting.

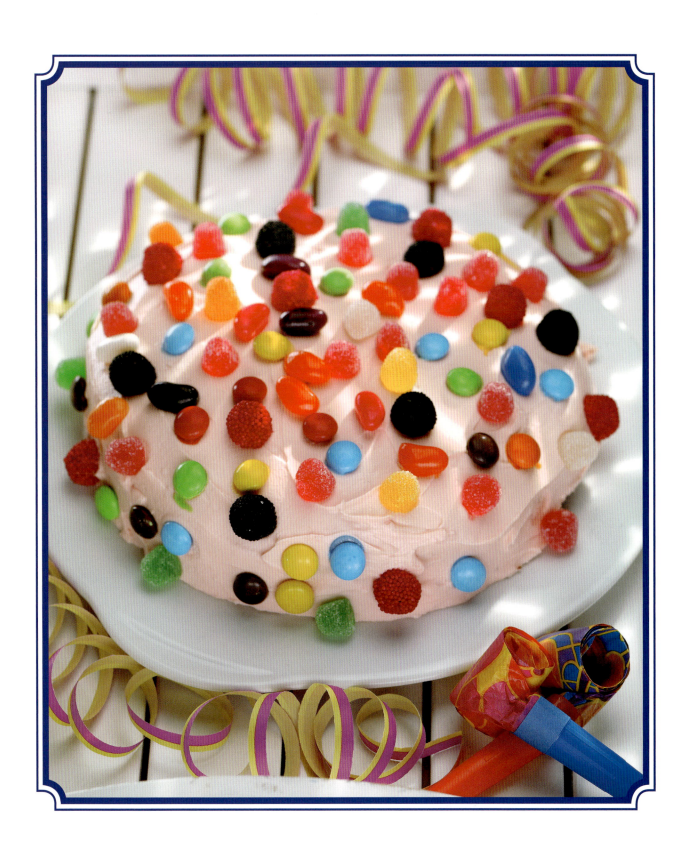

Chocolate Spider Cake

Serves 8-10

Chocolate Cake

½ cup (1 stick) unsalted buter

1¾ cups sugar

2 large eggs

¾ cup unsweetened cocoa

2 cups all-purpose flour

1½ teaspoons baking powder

1½ teaspoons baking soda

1 teaspoon salt

1 cup whole milk

2 teaspoons vanilla extract

1 cup boiling water

Dark Chocolate Frosting

1 cup (2 sticks) butter, softened

½ cup unsweetened cocoa

2¾ cups confectioners' sugar

½ cup whole milk

1 teaspoon vanilla extract

Decoration

½ cup white chocolate chips

1 teaspoon vegetable oil

Ready-roll marzipan

Red licorice string

2 small red and white candies

Directions

• Preheat the oven to 350°F. Lightly grease two 8-inch round cake pans, and line with parchment paper.

• Cream the butter and sugar together until smooth and light in color. Beat in one egg at a time, mixing well.

• Sift the cocoa, flour, baking powder, baking soda and salt into a separate bowl. Stir together and slowly add to the mixing bowl containing the creamed butter and sugar, mixing well. Finally add in the milk, vanilla extract. and water. Pour the mixture evenly into the pans. Place in the oven and bake for 30 minutes or until a toothpick inserted into the center comes out clean. Remove and cool before frosting.

• To make the frosting, beat the butter until fluffy, add in

cocoa, sugar and vanilla extract. Beat until creamy and add in milk until the right consistency has been reached. Sandwich the two cakes together with frosting and frost the outside of the cake.

• To make the web, place the white chocolate chips and vegetable oil in a small, zip-top plastic bag. Place in a microwave oven and cook on High for 45 seconds or until the chips have melted. Make a small diagonal cut in a bottom corner of the bag; squeeze the mixture onto the cake making a series of 4–5 circles. Using a toothpick draw 8–10 lines through the circles from the center to the edges of the cake to form the web.

• Shape some marzipan into the spider's body, and dust generously with cocoa. Use some red licorice string for legs and small red and white candies for eyes.

Flower Cake

Serves 8-10

Chocolate Cake

½ cup (1 stick) unsalted buter

1¾ cups sugar

2 large eggs

¾ cup unsweetened cocoa

2 cups all-purpose flour

1½ teaspoons baking powder

1½ teaspoons baking soda

1 teaspoon salt

1 cup whole milk

2 teaspoons vanilla extract

1 cup boiling water

Buttercream Frosting

1 cup unsalted butter, softened

5 cups confectioners' sugar

2-3 tablespoons whole milk

1 teaspoon vanilla extract

Decoration

Black licorice, to frame

Orange and green candy string, flower

Assorted gum drops and jelly candies

Directions

• Preheat the oven to 350°F. Lightly grease two 8-inch square cake pans and line with parchment paper.

• Cream the butter and sugar together until smooth and light in color. Beat in one egg at a time, mixing well.

• Sift the cocoa, flour, baking powder, baking soda and salt into a separate bowl. Stir together and slowly add to the mixing bowl containing the creamed butter and sugar, mixing well. Finally add in the milk, vanilla extract and water. Pour the mixture evenly into the pans. Place in the oven and bake for 30 minutes or until a toothpick inserted into the center comes out clean. Remove and cool.

• To make the frosting, beat the butter until fluffy and add the sugar, milk and vanilla, beating until pale and creamy. If the mixture seems too thin add more sugar. Sandwich the cakes together with the frosting and then cover the cake completely.

• Lay the licorice around the edge of the cake. Cut the orange candy string into pieces approximately 8 inches in length. Then outline the petals of a flower on the cake as shown. Use a long piece of green candy string to shape the stem. Cut two 2-inch pieces of the green string, placing them halfway along the stem to form small leaves. If desired, add 2 very short pieces of string to form the bud. Fill in the petals of the flower and the 2 stem leaves with sugar drop candies. Place the gummy candy in the middle of the blossom.

Berry Cake

Serves 8-10

Chocolate Cake

1 cup (2 sticks) unsalted buter

3 cups sugar

4 large eggs

1½ cups unsweetened cocoa

4 cups all-purpose flour

2 teaspoons baking powder

2 teaspoons baking soda

1 teaspoon salt

2 cups whole milk

2 teaspoons vanilla extract

1 cup boiling water

Chocolate Glaze

3 cups semisweet chocolate pieces

6 tablespoons vegetable shortening

Cream and Decoration

1 cup white chocolate chips

1 cup heavy cream

½ teaspoon vanilla extract

3 tablespoons confectioners' sugar

2 cups raspberries, rinsed and drained

Directions

• Preheat the oven to 350°F. Lightly grease one 9-inch round cake pan and one 8-inch round cake pan and line both with parchment paper.

• Cream the butter and sugar together until smooth and light in color. Beat in one egg at a time, mixing well.

• Sift the cocoa, flour, baking powder, baking soda and salt into a separate bowl. Stir together and slowly add to the mixing bowl containing the creamed butter and sugar, mixing well. Finally add in the milk, vanilla extract. and water. Pour the mixture evenly into the pans. Place in the oven and bake for 30 minutes or until a toothpick inserted into the center comes out clean. Remove and cool.

• Place the smaller cake on top of the larger one and coat with the glaze.

• To make the glaze, put the chocolate pieces and shortening in a glass bowl placed over a pan of simmering water. The chocolate will melt slowly. Stir regularly whilst melting.

• Pour the glaze over the cake. Decorate the surface of the cake with the white chocolate chips/ pieces and let cool.

• Shortly before serving, whip the cream to soft peaks, adding the vanilla extract and sugar. Spoon the whipped cream on top of the cake. Scatter the raspberries over the surface of the cake, and serve.

Rose Blossom Cake

Serves 8-10

Yogurt Sponge Cake

¾ cup (1½ sticks) unsalted buter

1½ cups sugar

3 large eggs

2 cups all-purpose flour

1 teaspoon baking powder

1 teaspoon baking soda

1 teaspoon salt

1 cup plain yogurt

2 teaspoons vanilla extract

1 teaspoon almond extract

Buttercream Frosting

1 cup (2 sticks) unsalted butter, softened

5 cups confectioners' sugar

2-3 tablespoons whole milk

1 teaspoon vanilla extract

Decoration

Red food coloring

1 pound 4 ounces ready-to-use

fondant icing

Crystallized rose petals

Directions

• Preheat the oven to 350°F.

• Grease one 6-inch and one 8-inch round cake pan and line with parchment paper.

• Cream the butter and the sugar until fluffy. Beat in the eggs, one at a time. Slowly sift in the the flour, baking powder, baking soda and salt.

• In a separate bowl mix the yogurt, vanilla and almond extract. Add slowly to the dry mixture, mixing until well blended. Pour into the prepared pans.

• Bake for 35 minutes or until a toothpick inserted into the center comes out clean. Leave to cool.

• To make the frosting, beat the butter until fluffy and add the sugar, milk and vanilla, beating until pale and creamy. If the mixture seems too thin add more sugar to thicken.

• Slice both cakes in half horizontally and add a layer of buttercream frosting. Lightly frost the sides and top of each cake separately.

• Dye the fondant pink by adding a very small drop of food coloring. Roll out to a large circle and smooth the icing over each. Trim. Place each cake on top of each other.

• Decorate the cakes with the crystallized rose leaves or cut some of the fondant icing into petal shapes.

Lace Cake

Serves 8-10

Chocolate Cake

1 cup (2 sticks) unsalted buter

3 cups sugar

4 large eggs

1½ cups unsweetened cocoa

4 cups all-purpose flour

2 teaspoons baking powder

2 teaspoons baking soda

1 teaspoon salt

2 cups whole milk

2 teaspoons vanilla extract

1 cup boiling water

Dark Chocolate Frosting

1 cup (2 sticks) unsalted butter, softened

¾ cup unsweetened cocoa

2¾ cups confectioners' sugar

½ cup whole milk

1 teaspoon vanilla extract

Decoration

¼ cup cocoa powder, for dusting

¼ cup confectioners' sugar, for dusting

One 8-inch round doily or plastic stencil

Chocolate-covered coffee beans

Silver candy balls

Directions

• Preheat the oven to 350°F. Lightly grease one 9-inch round cake pan and line with parchment paper.

• Cream the butter and sugar together until smooth and light in color. Beat in one egg at a time, mixing well.

• Sift together the cocoa, flour, baking powder, baking soda and salt into a separate bowl. Slowly add to the mixing bowl containing the creamed butter and sugar, mixing well. Finally add in the milk, vanilla extract. and water. Pour the mixture evenly into the pan.

• Place in the oven and bake for 30 minutes or until a toothpick inserted into the center comes out clean. Remove and cool.

• To make the frosting, beat the butter until fluffy. Sift together the cocoa and sugar and add to the butter, together with the milk and vanilla extract. Beat until creamy and spreadable.

• Slice the cake in half horizontally and sandwich together with the frosting.

• Just before serving, fill a small fine-mesh strainer with cocoa. Dust the cake by gently tapping as you move the strainer over the cake. Then place the doily or stencil on the cake, fill the strainer with confectioners' sugar and dust the cake. Carefully remove the doily—the lace pattern will show up on the cake.

• Decorate with coffee beans and silver balls.

Daisy Cake

Serves 8-10

Sour Cream Pound Cake

3 cups all-purpose flour

½ teaspoon baking powder

½ teaspoon baking soda

½ teaspoon salt

1 cup (2 sticks) unsalted butter

3 cups sugar

6 large eggs

1 teaspoon vanilla extract

1 teaspoon lemon extract

1 cup sour cream

Buttercream Frosting

1 cup (2 sticks) unsalted butter, softened

5 cups confectioners' sugar

2-3 tablespoons milk

1 teaspoon vanilla extract

Decoration

Yellow and red food coloring

Candy flowers

Candy buttons

Directions

• Preheat the oven to 350°F. Lightly grease two 8-inch round pans and line with parchment paper.

• Sift the flour, baking powder, baking soda and salt into a bowl. In a second bowl, beat the butter and sugar until fluffy and light. Beat in one egg at a time. Add the vanilla and lemon extract. Add the flour mixture, a little at a time, alternating with the sour cream. Mix well.

• Pour the batter into the pans and smooth it out evenly. Place the pans in the oven and bake for 35 minutes or until a toothpick comes out clean when inserted into the center of the cake. Leave to cool.

• To make the frosting, beat the butter until fluffy and add the sugar, milk and vanilla, beating until pale and creamy. If the mixture seems too thin add more sugar to thicken slightly.

• Dye the frosting with the yellow food coloring. Add a few drops of red for a slightly more orange shade. Sandwich the two cakes together with the frosting. Use the remaining frosting to cover the cake evenly. Use a knife to create a slightly wavy surface.

• Distribute the candy flowers on the top and sides of the cake and scatter the candy buttons over the surface.

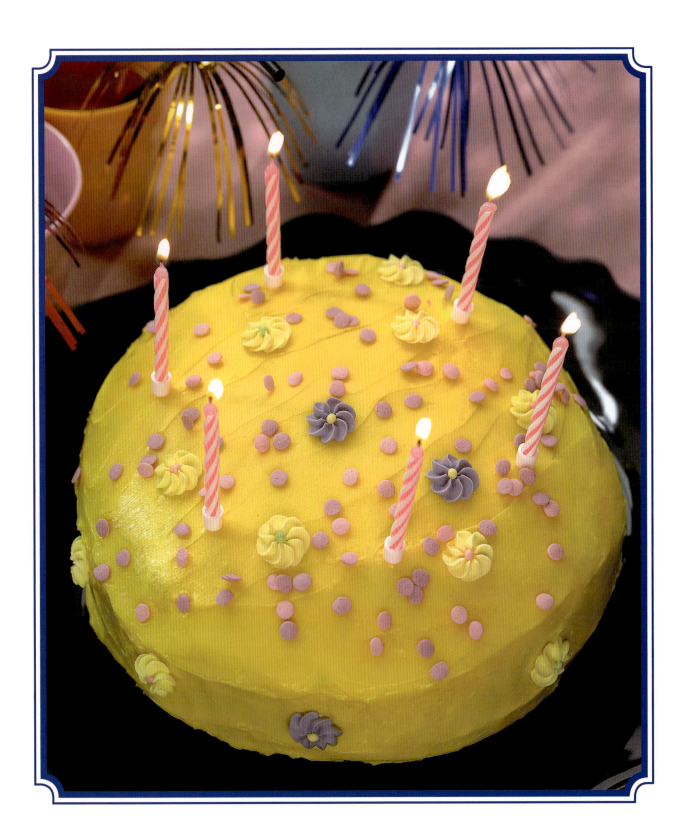

Balloon Cake

Serves 8-10

Yogurt Sponge Cake

¾ cup (1½ sticks) unsalted buter

1½ cups sugar

3 large eggs

1¾ cups all-purpose flour

1 teaspoon baking powder

1 teaspoon baking soda

1 teaspoon salt

1 cup plain yogurt

2 teaspoons vanilla extract

1 teaspoon almond extract

Buttercream Frosting

1 cup (2 sticks) unsalted butter, softened

5 cups confectioners' sugar

2-3 tablespoons whole milk

1 teaspoon vanilla extract

Decoration

Ready made marzipan

Food coloring, as needed

24-inch black licorice laces

Directions

• Preheat the oven to 350°F. Grease a 10-inch round cake pan and line with parchment paper.

• Cream the butter and the sugar until fluffy. Beat in the eggs, one at a time. Slowly sieve in the the flour, sugar, baking powder, baking soda and salt.

• In a separate bowl mix the yogurt, vanilla and almond extract. Add slowly to the cake mixture, mixing until well blended. Bake for 35 minutes or until a toothpick inserted into the center comes out clean. Leave to cool before frosting.

• To make the frosting, beat the butter until fluffy and add the sugar, milk and vanilla, beating until pale and creamy.

If the mixture seems too thin add more sugar to thicken.

• When the cake has cooled frost it using a palette knife to create an even surface.

• Create 3–5 different-colored marzipan mixtures by adding the food die to pieces of marzipan. Roll each piece of marzipan flat and shape them into circles or ovals. Place the pieces onto the cake. Cut the licorice string into 2-inch lengths and place them on the cake to create the balloon strings. Vary the lengths if desired. Decorate with a ribbon of marzipan around the cake.

Index

almonds
Almond Chocolate Biscotti 22
Almond & Raspberry Bars 190
Almond Slices 10
Apple & Cinnamon Bars 210
Blueberries & Cream Crumb Bars 38
Chocolate Fudge Cake 276
Fruit-tinis 76
Peach & Almond Pie 262
Raspberry & Chocolate Party Cups 34
Angel Food Cake 294
apples
Apple & Cinnamon Bars 210
Apple Cinnamon Swirl Bake 54
Blackberry & Apple Loaf Cake 160
Mixed Fruit Cookies 238
Simple Apple Pie 248
Spicy Apple Muffins 142
apricots
Apricot Bars 202
Apricot Crumble Cake 118
Fondue 62
Trail Mix Bar 194

banana pudding mix: Banana Trifle Cake 44
bananas
Banana & Chocolate Cookies 234
Banana & Cranberry Loaf Cake 158
Banana Crunch Cake 280
Banana Loaf Cake 156
Banana Muffins 138
bars
Almond & Raspberry Bars 190
Apple & Cinnamon Bars 210
Apricot Bars 202
Blueberries & Cream Crumb Bars 38
Chocolate Oat Bars 214
Chocolate Peppermint Bars 206
Cinnamon Raisin Bars 196
Dreamy Chocolate Bars 80
Lemon Drizzle Bars 192
Marshmallow Crunch Bars 216
No-Bake Chocolate Fingers 212
Nutty Granola Bars 204
Sticky Pecan Pie Bars 208
Trail Mix Bar 194
berries
Angel Food Cake 294
Coconut Cake with Spiced Berries 68
Fruit-tinis 76
Yummy Rummy Fruit Parfait 12
see also blackberries; blueberries; cranberries;
raspberries; strawberries
blackberries
Berry Bruschetta Cake Stacks 58
Blackberry & Apple Loaf Cake 160
Three Berry Pie 264
blueberries
Blueberries & Cream Crumb Bars 38
Blueberry & Cranberry Cookies 226

Blueberry Crumb Cake 122
Blueberry Muffin Supreme 128
Blueberry Sour Cream Loaf Cake 166
Fresh Blueberry Pie 260
Fruit Cobbler 16
Three Berry Pie 264
Brazil nuts
Chocolate Chiffon Tart 274
White Chocolate Cookies 230
brownies
Black & White Brownies 186
Chocolate Fudge Brownies 198
Cranberry Sour Cream Brownies 200
Double Chocolate Brownies 188
Brownies (Entenmann's)
Brownie Cheesecake 84
Cookie Brownies 48
Fruit-tinis 76
Little Bite Brownie Surprises 18
Little Bite Flying Saucers 36
S'more Party Cups 20

cakes
Angel Food Cake 294
Balloon Cake 316
Banana Crunch Cake 280
Berry Cake 308
Candy Store Cake 302
Carrot Cake 282
Cherry Fudge Cake 56
Chocolate Fudge Cake 276
Chocolate Spider Cake 304
Coffee & Walnut Swirl 278
Cookie Sour Cream Coffee Cake 24
Daisy Cake 314
Double Chocolate Mint Cake 288
Flower Cake 306
I Love You Cake 86
Lace Cake 312
Mocha Layer Cake 272
Pumpkin Sandwich Cake 292
Quick & Easy Birthday Cake 88
Rich Chocolate Layer Cake 284
Rose Blossom Cake 310
Strawberry Layer Cake 286
White Chocolate Mocha Cake 290
see also cheesecakes; crumb cakes; loaf cakes
caramel
Cafe Caramel Tiramisu 46
Caramel Breakfast Bake 28
carrots
Candy Store Cake 302
Carrot Cake 282
Carrot Cake Muffins 140
cashews: Dreamy Chocolate Bars 80
cheesecakes
Brownie Cheesecake 84, 298
New York Cheesecake 296
Raspberry & Chocolate Party Cups 34
cherries

Cherry Pie 250
Chocolate Cherry Trifle 60
Marshmallow Crunch Bars 216
No-Bake Chocolate Fingers 212
cherry pie filling
Cherry Fudge Cake 56
Chocolate Cherry Trifle 60
chocolate
Berry Cake 308
Black & White Brownies 186
Brownie Cheesecake 298
Cafe Caramel Tiramisu 46
Checkerboard Cookies 236
Cherry Fudge Cake 56
Chocolate Cake Donuts 106
Chocolate Chiffon Tart 274
Chocolate Fudge Brownies 198
Chocolate Fudge Cake 276
Chocolate Marshmallow Muffins 134
Chocolate & Orange Loaf Cake 174
Chocolate Peanut Butter Cups 66
Chocolate Peppermint Bars 206
Chocolate Pumpkin Pie 266
Chocolate Spider Cake 304
Cookie Truffles 32
Cranberry Sour Cream Brownies 200
Cream Eclairs 100
Double Chocolate Brownies 188
Double Chocolate Mint Cake 288
Double Chocolate Swirls 94
Fruit-tinis 76
I Love You Cake 86
Lace Cake 312
Little Bite Brownie Surprises 18
Marbled Loaf Cake 180
Midnight Cookies 228
Mississippi Mud Pie 254
Mocha Layer Cake 272
No-Bake Chocolate Fingers 212
Pumpkin Sandwich Cake 292
Raspberry & Chocolate Party Cups 34
Really Rich Chocolate Tartlets 258
Rich Chocolate Layer Cake 284
S'more Party Cups 20
White Chocolate Cookies 230
White Chocolate Mocha Cake 290
chocolate chip cookies (Entenmann's)
Chocolate Chip Icebox Cake 82
Coffee Toffee Ice Cream Pie 14
Cookie Brownies 48
Cookie Milkshake 26
Cookie Sour Cream Coffee Cake 24
Cookie Truffles 32
chocolate chips
Almond Chocolate Biscotti 22
Banana & Chocolate Cookies 234
Banana Trifle Cake 44
Chocolate Chip Cookies 232
Chocolate Chip Loaf Cake 162
Chocolate Oat Bars 214

Chocolate Peanut Butter Loaf Cake 172
Double Chocolate Brownies 188
Double Chocolate Chip Muffins 130
Dreamy Chocolate Bars 80
Fondue 62
Marshmallow Crunch Bars 216
Chocolate Fudge Cake (Entenmann's)
    Cherry Fudge Cake 56
    Chocolate Peanut Butter Cups 66
chocolate pudding mix
    Chocolate Cherry Trifle 60
    Festive Loaf Cake 42
Cinnamon Crumb Cake 114
Cinnamon Raisin Bars 196
Cinnamon Raisin Loaf Cake 176
Cinnamon Swirl Rolls 104
coconut
    Apricot Crumble Cake 118
    Candy Store Cake 302
    Coconut Cake with Spiced Berries 68
    Dreamy Chocolate Bars 80
coffee
    Cafe Caramel Tiramisu 46
    Chocolate Chip Loaf Cake 162
    Coffee Toffee Ice Cream Pie 14
    Coffee & Walnut Swirl 278
    Mocha Layer Cake 272
    White Chocolate Mocha Cake 290
cookies
    Banana & Chocolate Cookies 234
    Blueberry & Cranberry Cookies 226
    Checkerboard Cookies 236
    Chocolate Chip Cookies 232
    Midnight Cookies 228
    Mixed Fruit Cookies 238
    Oatmeal, Raisin & Nut Cookies 222
    Peanut Butter Cookies 220
    Vanilla Sugar Cookies 224
    White Chocolate Cookies 230
cranberries
    Banana & Cranberry Loaf Cake 158
    Blueberry & Cranberry Cookies 226
    Cranberry Sour Cream Brownies 200
    Orange & Cranberry Muffins 132
cream cheese
    Banana Crunch Cake 280
    Black & White Brownies 186
    Brownie Cheesecake 84, 298
    Candy Store Cake 302
    Carrot Cake 282
    Carrot Cake Muffins 140
    Chocolate Chip Icebox Cake 82
    Cinnamon Swirl Rolls 104
    Cookie Truffles 32
    Cream Cheese Swirl Coffee Cake 116
    Frosted Cream Cheese Muffins 144
    New York Cheesecake 296
    Pumpkin Sandwich Cake 292
    see also mascarpone cheese; ricotta cheese
Crumb Cake (Entenmann's)
    Fruit Cobbler 16
    Stuffed French Crumb Cake 64
crumb cakes
Apricot Crumble Cake 118
    Blueberry Crumb Cake 122
    Cinnamon Crumb Cake 114

Cream Cheese Swirl Coffee Cake 116
    Pumpkin Crumb Cake 120

Danish
    Cinnamon Swirl Rolls 104
    Double Chocolate Swirls 94
Date & Walnut Loaf Cake 170
donuts
    Chocolate Cake Donuts 106
    Jelly Donuts 96
    Simple Donuts 92
    Sour Cream Donuts 102
    Spiced Donut Holes 110
    Donuts (Entenmann's)
    Berry Cakes 78
    Blueberries & Cream Crumb Bars 38
    Cafe Caramel Tiramisu 46
    Donut Pudding with Zabaglione 70
    Dreamy Chocolate Bars 80

fondant
    Quick & Easy Birthday Cake 88
    Rose Blossom Cake 310
Fondue 62

ginger, candied
    Coconut Cake with Spiced Berries 68
    Ginger Loaf Cake 182
graham crackers
    Chocolate Pumpkin Pie 266
    Key Lime Pie 256
    New York Cheesecake 296
    No-Bake Chocolate Fingers 212
    S'more Party Cups 20

hazelnut spread: Double Chocolate Swirls 94
hazelnuts
    Nutty Granola Bars 204
    Oatmeal, Raisin & Nut Cookies 222
    Three Berry Pie 264
honey
    Apricot Bars 202
    Trail Mix Bar 194

ice cream
    Coffee Toffee Ice Cream Pie 14
    Cookie Milkshake 26
    Donut Pudding with Zabaglione 70
    Lady Georgia Cake 72
    Little Bite Flying Saucers 36
Iced Cake (Entenmann's)
    I Love You Cake 86
    Quick & Easy Birthday Cake 88

jellies & preserves
    Almond & Raspberry Bars 190
    Apricot Crumble Cake 118
    Berry Bruschetta Cake Stacks 58
    Berry Cakes 78
    Fruit Turnovers 98
    Jelly Donut Mufins 136
    Jelly Donuts 96
    Raspberry & Chocolate Party Cups 34

lemons
    Blueberry Sour Cream Loaf Cake 166

Frosted Cream Cheese Muffins 144
    Lemon Drizzle Bars 192
    Lemon Loaf Cake 152
    Lemon Meringue Pie 242
    Lemon Poppy Seed Muffins 126
    Lemon Sponge Pie 268
    Loaf Cake with Orange Glaze 154
    New York Cheesecake 296
limes: Key Lime Pie 256
Loaf Cake (Entenmann's)
    A Pound of French Cake 40
    Almond Chocolate Biscotti 22
    Almond Slices 10
    Banana Trifle Cake 44
    Berry Bruschetta Cake Stacks 58
    Caramel Breakfast Bake 28
    Chocolate Cherry Trifle 60
    Coconut Cake with Spiced Berries 68
    Easy Baklava 30
    Festive Loaf Cake 42
    Fondue 62
    Lady Georgia Cake 72
    Meringue Cake 50
    Strawberry Loaf Cake 52
    Yummy Rummy Fruit Parfait 12
loaf cakes
    Banana & Cranberry Loaf Cake 158
    Banana Loaf Cake 156
    Blackberry & Apple Loaf Cake 160
    Blueberry Sour Cream Loaf Cake 166
    Brown Sugar Walnut Loaf Cake 178
    Chocolate Chip Loaf Cake 162
    Chocolate & Orange Loaf Cake 174
    Chocolate Peanut Butter Loaf Cake 172
    Cinnamon Raisin Loaf Cake 176
    Date & Walnut Loaf Cake 170
    Ginger Loaf Cake 182
    Lemon Loaf Cake 152
    Loaf Cake with Orange Glaze 154
    Marbled Loaf Cake 180
    Poppy Seed Loaf Cake 168
    Pound Loaf Cake 164

mangoes: Meringue Cake 50
maple syrup: Almond Slices 10
Marbled Loaf Cake 180
marshmallow crème
    Blueberries & Cream Crumb Bars 38
    Festive Loaf Cake 42
    S'more Party Cups 20
marshmallows
    Chocolate Marshmallow Muffins 134
    Fondue 62
    Marshmallow Crunch Bars 216
mascarpone cheese
    Cafe Caramel Tiramisu 46
    Strawberry Layer Cake 286
Mississippi Mud Pie 254
Mocha Layer Cake 272
muffins
    Banana Muffins 138
    Blueberry Muffin Supreme 128
    Carrot Cake Muffins 140
    Chocolate Marshmallow Muffins 134
    Double Chocolate Chip Muffins 130
    Frosted Cream Cheese Muffins 144

Jelly Donut Mufins 136
Lemon Poppy Seed Muffins 126
Muffin Pudding 74
Orange & Cranberry Muffins 132
Raspberry Crumble Muffins 146
Sour Cream Muffins 148
Spicy Apple Muffins 142

New York Cheesecake 296
nuts
Banana & Cranberry Loaf Cake 158
Chocolate Oat Bars 214
Easy Baklava 30
Marshmallow Crunch Bars 216
see also almonds; Brazil nuts; cashews; hazelnuts;
peanut butter; pecans; walnuts

oats
Apricot Bars 202
Chocolate Oat Bars 214
Cinnamon Raisin Bars 196
Nutty Granola Bars 204
Oatmeal, Raisin & Nut Cookies 222
Peanut Butter Cookies 220
Pumpkin Crumb Cake 120
Spicy Apple Muffins 142
Trail Mix Bar 194
oranges
Banana & Cranberry Loaf Cake 158
Banana Loaf Cake 156
Banana Muffins 138
Carrot Cake 282
Carrot Cake Muffins 140
Checkerboard Cookies 236
Chocolate & Orange Loaf Cake 174
Loaf Cake with Orange Glaze 154
Mixed Fruit Cookies 238
New York Cheesecake 296
Orange & Cranberry Muffins 132

pastries
Cream Eclairs 100
Cream Puffs 108
Fruit Turnovers 98
peaches
A Pound of French Cake 40
Fruit Cobbler 16
Lady Georgia Cake 72
Peach & Almond Pie 262
peanut butter
Chocolate Peanut Butter Cups 66
Chocolate Peanut Butter Loaf Cake 172
Muffin Pudding 74
Peanut Butter Cookies 220
Trail Mix Bar 194
pears: Mixed Fruit Cookies 238
pecan syrup: A Pound of French Cake 40
pecans
Banana Crunch Cake 280
Brownie Cheesecake 84
Carrot Cake 282
Carrot Cake Muffins 140
Lady Georgia Cake 72
Pecan Pie 252
Spiced Pumpkin Pie 246
Sticky Pecan Pie Bars 208

peppermint
Chocolate Peppermint Bars 206
Double Chocolate Mint Cake 288
pies
Candied Sweet Potato Pie 244
Cherry Pie 250
Chocolate Chiffon Tart 274
Chocolate Pumpkin Pie 266
Coffee Toffee Ice Cream Pie 14
Fresh Blueberry Pie 260
Key Lime Pie 256
Lemon Meringue Pie 242
Lemon Sponge Pie 268
Mississippi Mud Pie 254
Peach & Almond Pie 262
Pecan Pie 252
Really Rich Chocolate Tartlets 258
Simple Apple Pie 248
Spiced Pumpkin Pie 246
Three Berry Pie 264
pine nuts: Blueberry & Cranberry Cookies 226
pineapple
Banana Crunch Cake 280
Candy Store Cake 302
Yummy Rummy Fruit Parfait 12
popcorn: Dreamy Chocolate Bars 80
poppy seeds
Lemon Poppy Seed Muffins 126
Poppy Seed Loaf Cake 168
Pound Loaf Cake 164
prunes: Mixed Fruit Cookies 238
pumpkin
Chocolate Pumpkin Pie 266
Pumpkin Crumb Cake 120
Pumpkin Sandwich Cake 292
Spiced Pumpkin Pie 246

raisins
Apple Cinnamon Swirl Bake 54
Banana & Chocolate Cookies 234
Banana Muffins 138
Carrot Cake Muffins 140
Cinnamon Raisin Bars 196
Cinnamon Raisin Loaf Cake 176
Donut Pudding with Zabaglione 70
Oatmeal, Raisin & Nut Cookies 222
raspberries
Almond & Raspberry Bars 190
Berry Bruschetta Cake Stacks 58
Berry Cake 308
Berry Cakes 78
I Love You Cake 86
Raspberry & Chocolate Party Cups 34
Raspberry Crumble Muffins 146
Three Berry Pie 264
ricotta cheese: Cream Puffs 108

seeds, edible see pine nuts; poppy seeds; sesame
seeds
sesame seeds
Apricot Bars 202
Trail Mix Bar 194
sour cream
Blueberry Crumb Cake 122
Blueberry Muffin Supreme 128
Blueberry Sour Cream Loaf Cake 166

Cinnamon Crumb Cake 114
Cookie Sour Cream Coffee Cake 24
Cranberry Sour Cream Brownies 200
Cream Cheese Swirl Coffee Cake 116
Daisy Cake 314
Frosted Cream Cheese Muffins 144
Marbled Loaf Cake 180
Sour Cream Donuts 102
Sour Cream Muffins 148
White Chocolate Mocha Cake 290
strawberries
Berry Bruschetta Cake Stacks 58
Berry Cakes 78
Cream Puffs 108
Fondue 62
Strawberry Layer Cake 286
Strawberry Loaf Cake 52
sweet potatoes: Candied Sweet Potato Pie 244

toffee
Coffee Toffee Ice Cream Pie 14
Little Bite Brownie Surprises 18
Trail Mix Bar 194

vanilla pudding
Fruit-tinis 76
Stuffed French Crumb Cake 64
Vanilla Sugar Cookies 224

walnuts
Brown Sugar Walnut Loaf Cake 178
Candy Store Cake 302
Carrot Cake Muffins 140
Chocolate Chip Cookies 232
Chocolate Fudge Brownies 198
Coffee & Walnut Swirl 278
Cookie Sour Cream Coffee Cake 24
Cream Cheese Swirl Coffee Cake 116
Date & Walnut Loaf Cake 170
Pumpkin Crumb Cake 120
Spiced Pumpkin Pie 246

yogurt
Balloon Cake 316
Blackberry & Apple Loaf Cake 160
Raspberry Crumble Muffins 146
Rose Blossom Cake 310